The Contemporary
Cake Decorating Bible

Over 150 techniques and 80 stunning projects

Lindy Smith

W/D SALE

D&C

David and Charles

A DAVID & CHARLES BOOK
© F&W Media International, LTD 2011

David & Charles is an imprint of F&W Media International, LTD
Brunel House, Forde Close, Newton Abbot, TQ12 4PU, UK

F&W Media International, LTD is a subsidiary of F+W Media, Inc.
4700 East Galbraith Road, Cincinnati, OH 45236

First published in the UK and USA in 2011

Text and designs © Lindy Smith 2011
Layout and photography © F&W Media International, LTD 2011

Lindy Smith has asserted her right to be identified as author of this work in accordance with the Copyright, Designs and Patents Act, 1988.

All rights reserved. No part of this publication may be reproduced, stored in a retrieval system, or transmitted, in any form or by any means, electronic or mechanical, by photocopying, recording or otherwise, without prior permission in writing from the publisher.

Readers are permitted to reproduce any of the patterns or designs in this book for their personal use and without the prior permission of the publisher. However the designs in this book are copyright and must not be reproduced for resale.

The author and publisher have made every effort to ensure that all the instructions in the book are accurate and safe, and therefore cannot accept liability for any resulting injury, damage or loss to persons or property, however it may arise.

Names of manufacturers and product ranges are provided for the information of readers, with no intention to infringe copyright or trademarks.

A catalogue record for this book is available from the British Library.

ISBN-13: 978-0-7153-3836-0 hardback
ISBN-10: 0-7153-3836-6 hardback

ISBN-13: 978-0-7153-3837-7 paperback
ISBN-10: 0-7153-3837-4 paperback

Printed in Italy by G.Canale & C. S.p.A.
for F&W Media International LTD,
Brunel House, Forde Close, Newton Abbot, TQ12 4PU, UK

10 9 8 7 6 5 4 3 2 1

Publisher Alison Myer
Acquisitions Editor Jenifer Fox-Proverbs
Editor James Brooks
Project Editor Ame Verso
Art Editor Charly Bailey
Photographer Karl Adamson and Simon Whitmore
Senior Production Controller Kelly Smith

F+W Media Inc. publishes high quality books on a wide range of subjects. For more great book ideas visit: www.rucraft.co.uk

LIBRARIES NI	
C900228133	
Bertrams	26/02/2012
641.86539	£19.99
LURGRP	

Contents

Introduction

When my publishers asked me to write this book, I simply couldn't resist. Despite the tight deadlines for such a large book I could not refuse, for I knew this book needed to be written and I wanted to be the one to do it! My cake mission has always been to inspire others and to bring a contemporary look to sugarcraft design.

I have thoroughly enjoyed the creative process in putting this book together. It has been a wonderful voyage of discovery, a journey I didn't want to end. I have included many of the techniques that I frequently use on my own cakes and cookies. I have not been able to include every possible technique, but I am convinced that by using this book you will be able to create gorgeous cakes with ease.

Contemporary well-decorated cakes impress everyone – whether they are dainty cupcakes, mini-cakes or large multi-tiered creations. Cakes don't have to be complicated. Simple embossing, using cut-out shapes, moulds or stencils are quick, effective techniques that can be used to create stunning cakes. My advice is to start small – cupcakes and cookies are nowhere near as daunting as large cakes.

Ever since I started cake decorating, I have always strived to create contemporary cakes. Growing up I was encouraged, especially by my grandmother, to look around me to see what was current… to be 'on trend'! Today, I gain inspiration from what I am attracted to in the world around me. I then interpret these images in my own way into my cake designs. I am essentially an artist and my medium is sugar.

Inspiration for the designs in this book came from many sources: interior design, art nouveau stained glass, wrought-iron work, art exhibitions, bed linen, clothing fabrics, upholstery, jewellery designs and floral art. I admire the work of artists such as Wassily Kandinsky, architects like Antoni Gaudi and fashion designers like Valentino. Colour is key to a contemporary look. Fashionable colours and colour combinations come and go. However, the simplest way for a cake to look modern is to use colours that you see all around you in magazines, catalogues, fabrics, fashion, window displays, stationery, bedding and so on.

Like most art forms, when you start cake decorating you learn by copying other cakes. However, as your confidence grows you will feel able to branch out with your own ideas. I am hoping that this book will enable you to do this. To make a contemporary cake today is much simpler than ever before because there is a fantastic selection of specialist equipment readily available to help you. This equipment is not essential by any means, but it does help you achieve striking results more easily.

Experiment, have fun, create something wonderful and unique. Look at the world around you for inspiration and follow the detailed techniques in this book to transfer your ideas successfully onto fabulous cakes and cookies. And do let me know how you get on via the Lindy's Cakes Facebook page or blog. Enjoy and happy cake creating!

Lindy

www.lindyscakes.co.uk

★ How to use this book

This book covers all the basics in the introductory section including equipment, cake and sugar recipes, covering cakes, boards and cookies, stacking, storing and cutting cakes. The main section of the book is then divided into technique chapters, which concentrate on one aspect of cake decorating at a time. Each chapter is filled with examples to inspire you plus one main cake that uses one or more of the techniques from that chapter. At the back of the book you will find a dedicated Projects chapter, where you will find a list of the tools, cutters and equipment I have used to create all the cakes and cookies shown in the book, plus a brief description of the techniques used.

Preparation and Planning

Although you will be keen to start experimenting with the techniques in this book, take the time to read this section so that you are familiar with the fundamentals of cake decorating. This will help make your cakes and cookies look more professional, whatever technique you use. Try not to leave everything to the last minute – plan your decorating time in advance, allowing time for experimentation.

Equipment

You will find the following lists of equipment useful when baking and decorating cakes and cookies. The first list contains general cake baking and decorating items while following lists give items needed to bake cupcakes, mini-cakes and cookies. Equipment specific to a particular technique, such as embossers, stencils, moulds and so on can be found in the relevant chapters throughout the book.

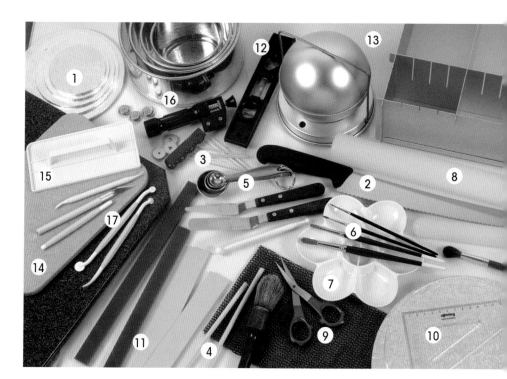

★ For general cake baking and decorating

1 Cake boards
   • Drum – 12mm (½in) thick board to display cakes
   • Hardboard – a thin strong board, usually the same size as the cake, which is placed under cake to act as a barrier and to give stability to stacked cakes
2 Carving knife – a sharp long-bladed pastry knife, for levelling cakes and carving shapes
3 Cocktail sticks (toothpicks) – used as markers and to transfer small amounts of edible paste colour
4 Dowels – used in conjunction with hardboards to support tiered cakes
5 Measuring spoons – for accurate measurement of ingredients
6 Paintbrushes – a range of sizes is useful for stippling, painting and dusting
7 Paint palette – for mixing edible paste colours and dusts prior to painting and dusting
8 Rolling pin – for rolling out the different types of paste
9 Scissors – for cutting templates and trimming paste to shape
10 Set square – for accurate alignment

11 Spacers – 1.5mm (¹⁄₁₆in) narrow and 5mm (³⁄₁₆in) for rolling out paste
12 Spirit level – to check dowels are vertical and tops of cakes are horizontal
13 Tins (pans) – for baking cakes – ball, round and multi-sized
14 Non-stick work board – for rolling out pastes
15 Smoother – to give a smooth and even finish to sugarpaste
16 Sugar shaper and discs – to create pieces of uniformly shaped modelling paste
17 Modelling tools
   • Ball tool (FMM) – gives even indentations in paste and softens the edges of petals
   • Craft knife – for intricate cutting tasks
   • Cutting wheel (PME) – use instead of a knife to avoid dragging the paste
   • Dresden tool – to create markings on paste
   • Palette knife – for cutting paste and spreading royal icing
   • Quilting tool (PME) – for adding stitching lines
   • Scriber (PME) – for scribing around templates, popping air bubbles in paste and removing small sections of paste

★ For cupcakes

1 Cupcake cases
2 Cupcake pans
3 Cupcake wrappers
4 Cupcake boxes
5 Large piping tubes (tips)
6 Round pastry cutters
7 Wire rack

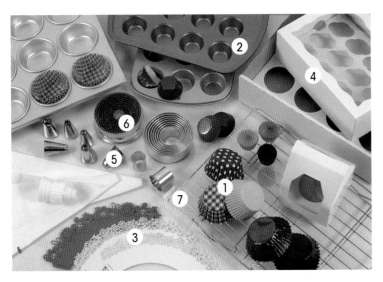

★ For mini-cakes

1 Multi mini tins
2 Small hardboard
 cake boards
3 Wire rack
4 Baking parchment

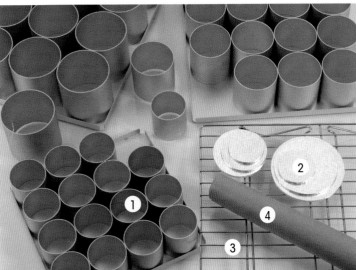

★ For cookies

1 Cookie cutters
2 Baking tray
3 Wire rack
4 Large palette knife
5 Clear cookie bags

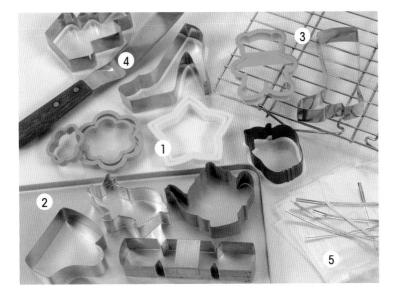

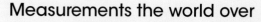

Measurements the world over

For those who prefer to use cups, please use the following conversions (1 tbsp = 15ml; 1 Australian tbsp = 20ml).

★ **Butter** 100g (3½oz) = 1 stick, 225g (8oz) = 1 cup, 25g (1oz) = 2 tbsp, 15g (½oz) = 1 tbsp

★ **Caster (superfine) sugar** 200g (7oz) = 1 cup, 25g (1oz) = 2 tbsp

★ **Desiccated (dry unsweetened shredded) coconut** 75g (3oz) = 1 cup, 4 tbsp = 25g (1oz)

★ **Dried fruit** 1 cup = currants 225g (8oz), raisins 150g (5oz), sultanas 175g (6oz)

★ **Flour** 150g (5oz) = 1 cup

★ **Glacé (candied) cherries** 225g (8oz) = 1 cup

★ **Icing (confectioners') sugar** 115g (4oz) = 1 cup

★ **Liquid** 250ml (9fl oz) = 1 cup, 125ml (4fl oz) = ½ cup

★ **Nuts, chopped or ground** 115g (4oz) = 1 cup

★ **Soft brown sugar** 115g (4oz) = 1 cup

Piping tubes (tips)

The following piping tubes have been used in the book. As tube numbers vary with different suppliers, always check the tube diameter.

Tube no. (PME)	Diameter
0	0.5mm (0.020in)
1	1mm (1⁄32in)
1.5	1.2mm (1⁄32in)
2	1.5mm (1⁄16in)
3	2mm (3⁄32in)
4	3mm (1⁄8in)
16	5mm (3⁄16in)
17	6mm (1⁄4in)
18	7mm (1⁄4in)

Lining cake tins (pans)

There are cake release sprays on the market but I prefer the traditional method of lining tins. Neatly lined tins will prevent the cake sticking and ensure a good shape. Use good-quality baking parchment designed for the purpose. The paper should sit right up against the sides with no large air pockets. Secure the upper edge of the paper with fat or a small fold to prevent it going into the cake.

Straight-sided tins

★ **Square, rectangular and hexagonal**

Measure the circumference of the tin and cut a strip of parchment slightly longer than this to allow for an overlap. Make the strip 5cm (2in) deeper than the height of the tin. Fold up 2.5cm (1in) along the bottom. Crease the strip at intervals the length of each inside edge then cut the folded section where it is creased into mitres. Grease the tin and place the strip around the sides with the cut edge on the base (**A**). Cut a piece of parchment to fit the base.

★ **Round and other curved shapes**

Line as above, however make diagonal cuts in the folded over section of the paper to enable it to sit snugly around the inside of the tin (**B**).

Multi mini tins

Line the base of the pan with a square of paper, then cut strips slightly longer than the circumference of each tin and slightly higher. Place one paper strip inside each tin so that the sides of the strip overlap a little (**C**).

Ball tins

Cut two circles from baking parchment: 15cm (6in) for a 10cm (4in) ball; 20cm (8in) for a 13cm (5in) ball; 25.5cm (10in) for a 15cm (6in) ball. Fold the circles into quarters to find the centres. Open out and make radial cuts into the circle. Grease the tin and one side of the paper and place into one half of the tin, greased sides together. Overlap the sections until it fits snugly (**D**).

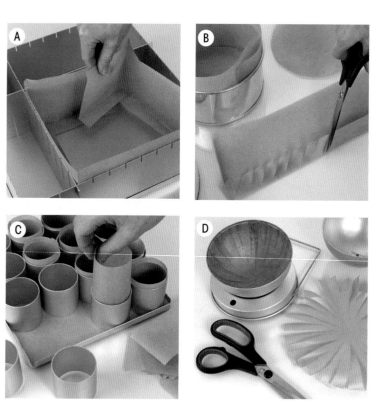

Baking Cakes

Following are my tried-and-tested recipes for chocolate cake, fruit cake and Madeira cake. A stacked cake can be made from just one type, or you could use sponge and fruit cake in different tiers.

Chocolate cake

This is a rich, moist, yet firm chocolate cake, ideal for both carving and covering with sugarpaste. The secret to this recipe is to use good-quality chocolate with a reasonably high cocoa solids content. Don't be tempted to use cheap, low cocoa solids chocolate or even supermarket baking chocolate – you simply will not achieve the depth of flavour this cake demands! This cake will keep for up to two weeks.

Chocolate cake quantities

Cake sizes		Plain (semisweet) chocolate	Unsalted (sweet) butter	Caster (superfine) sugar	Eggs (large) (US extra large)	Icing (confectioners') sugar	Self-raising (self-rising) flour	Baking times at 180°C/ 350°F/Gas 4
10cm (4in) round/ball	7.5cm (3in) square	75g (3oz)	50g (2oz)	40g (1½oz)	2	15g (½oz)	40g (1½oz)	30–45 mins
13cm (5in) round	10cm (4in) square	125g (4½oz)	75g (3oz)	50g (2oz)	3	20g (¾oz)	75g (3oz)	45 mins–1 hour
15cm (6in) round	13cm (5in) square/ball	175g (6oz)	115g (4oz)	75g (3oz)	4	25g (1oz)	115g (4oz)	45 mins–1 hour
18cm (7in) round	15cm (6in) square	225g (8oz)	175g (6oz)	115g (4oz)	6	40g (1½oz)	175g (6oz)	1–1¼ hours
20cm (8in) round	18cm (7in) square/15cm (6in) ball	275g (10oz)	225g (8oz)	150g (5oz)	8	50g (2oz)	225g (8oz)	1–1¼ hours
23cm (9in) round	20cm (8in) square	425g (15oz)	275g (10oz)	175g (6oz)	10	70g (2½oz)	275g (10oz)	1¼–1½ hours
25.5cm (10in) round	23cm (9in) square	500g (1lb 2oz)	350g (12oz)	225g (8oz)	12	75g (3oz)	350g (12oz)	1½–1¾ hours
28cm (11in) round	25.5cm (10in) square	550g (1¼lb)	450g (1lb)	275g (10oz)	16	115g (4oz)	450g (1lb)	1¾–2 hours
30cm (12in) round	28cm (11in) square	675g (1lb 7oz)	550g (1¼lb)	375g (13oz)	20	125g (4½oz)	550g (1¼lb)	2–2¼ hours
33cm (13in) round	30cm (12in) square	850g (1lb 14oz)	675g (1lb 7oz)	450g (1lb)	24	150g (5oz)	675g (1lb 7oz)	2¼–2¾ hours
35.5cm (14in) round	33cm (14in) square	1kg (2¼lb)	800g (1¾lb)	500g (1lb 2oz)	28	200g (7oz)	800g (1¾lb)	2½–2¾ hours

1 Preheat the oven to 180°C/350°F/Gas 4. Grease and line the cake tin (pan) with baking parchment.

2 Melt the chocolate, either in a heatproof bowl over a pan of boiling water or in a microwave. Cream the butter and sugar in a large mixing bowl until light, fluffy and pale.

3 Separate the eggs. Gradually add the egg yolks, then the melted chocolate. In a separate bowl, whisk the egg whites to soft peaks. Gradually whisk the icing (confectioners') sugar into the egg whites.

4 Sift the flour into another bowl and, using a large metal spoon, fold the flour alternately with the egg whites into the chocolate and egg yolk mixture.

5 Transfer the mixture into the lined bakeware and bake. Baking times will depend on your oven, the cake tin (pan) used and the depth of the cake. I usually check small cakes after 30 minutes, medium-sized cakes after an hour, and large cakes after two hours. When the cake is baked it will be well risen, firm to the touch and a skewer inserted into the centre will come out clean.

6 Allow the cake to cool completely in the tin, then, leaving the lining paper on, wrap the cake in foil or place in an airtight container for at least 12 hours before cutting to allow the cake to settle.

Fruit cake

Rich fruit cake is a wonderful traditional cake packed full of candied and dried fruit, usually soaked in spirits, plus nuts and spices. The quality of the fruit you use will make a huge difference to the flavour of your cake, so shop around to source the best you can find – candied peel that you have to chop yourself is always so much tastier!

Fruit cake should be aged for at least one month to allow the flavour to mature. Fruit wedding cakes are traditionally stored for at least three months to

give them a nicely matured flavour and to enable the cake to be cut cleanly into small portions. Young fruit cake will still be delicious but is difficult to cut neatly, which although fine for a family birthday, would not be suitable for a wedding.

If you prefer not to use spirits in your cake, try substituting apple or orange juice, or try grape or pomegranate juice. Without the alcohol preservative the cake won't have as long a shelf life but a non-alcoholic fruitcake will still last for quite a while.

Fruit cake quantities

Cake sizes		10cm (4in) round/ball	13cm (5in) round	15cm (6in) round	18cm (7in) round	20cm (8in) round	23cm (9in) round
		7.5cm (3in) square	10cm (4in) square	13cm (5in) square/ball	15cm (6in) square	18cm (7in) square/ 15cm (6in) ball	20cm (8in) square
Sultanas (golden raisins)		50g (2oz)	75g (3oz)	115g (4oz)	175g (6oz)	225g (8oz)	275g (10oz)
Currants		50g (2oz)	75g (3oz)	115g (4oz)	175g (6oz)	225g (8oz)	275g (10oz)
Raisins		50g (2oz)	75g (3oz)	115g (4oz)	175g (6oz)	225g (8oz)	275g (10oz)
Chopped peel		25g (1oz)	40g (1½oz)	50g (2oz)	75g (3oz)	115g (4oz)	150g (5oz)
Brandy		7.5ml (1½ tsp)	11.5ml (2¼ tsp)	15ml (1 tbsp)	25ml (1½ tbsp)	30ml (2 tbsp)	37.5ml (2½ tbsp)
Plain (all-purpose) flour		50g (2oz)	75g (3oz)	115g (4oz)	175g (6oz)	225g (8oz)	275g (10oz)
Ground almonds		15g (½oz)	20g (¾oz)	25g (1oz)	40g (1½oz)	50g (2oz)	70g (2½oz)
Mixed spice (apple pie)		1.5ml (¼ tsp)	2.5ml (½ tsp)	2.5ml (½ tsp)	3.5ml (¾ tsp)	5ml (1 tsp)	6.5ml (1¼ tsp)
Butter		50g (2oz)	75g (3oz)	115g (4oz)	175g (6oz)	225g (8oz)	275g (10oz)
Soft brown sugar		50g (2oz)	75g (3oz)	115g (4oz)	175g (6oz)	225g (8oz)	275g (10oz)
Eggs		1	1½	2	3	4	5
Black treacle (molasses)		2.5ml (½ tsp)	5ml (1 tsp)	7.5ml (1½ tsp)	15ml (1 tbsp)	15ml (1 tbsp)	20ml (4 tsp)
Vanilla extract		a few drops	1.5ml (¼ tsp)	1.5ml (¼ tsp)	2.5ml (½ tsp)	2.5ml (½ tsp)	3.5ml (¾ tsp)
Glacé (candied) cherries		25g (1oz)	40g (1½oz)	50g (2oz)	75g (3oz)	115g (4oz)	150g (5oz)
Chopped almonds		15g (½oz)	20g (¾oz)	25g (1oz)	40g (1½oz)	50g (2oz)	70g (2½oz)
Lemon rind and juice		¼	⅓	½	¾	1	1¼
Cooking times (approx)	150ºC/ 300ºF/ Gas 2	30 mins	30 mins	50 mins	1 hour	1½ hours	1¾ hours
	120ºC/ 250ºF/ Gas ½	30 mins	1 hour	1 hour 40 mins	2¼ hours	2½ hours	3¼ hours
Total		1 hour	1½ hours	2½ hours	3¼ hours	4 hours	5 hours

1 Soak the sultanas, currants, raisins and peel in brandy (or fruit juice) overnight.

2 Preheat the oven to 150°C/300°F/Gas 2. Sieve the flour, spice and almonds into a bowl. In another bowl cream the butter and sugar until light, pale and fluffy. Do not overbeat.

3 Mix together the eggs, treacle and vanilla. Beat into the creamed mixture a little at a time adding a spoonful of flour after each addition.

4 Rinse the cherries and chop. Add to the fruit with the lemon rind and juice, chopped almonds and a small amount of flour. Fold the remaining flour into the creamed mixture, followed by the dried fruit. Add extra brandy or milk if necessary.

5 Spoon into a lined cake tin (pan), level the top, and then slightly hollow the centre. Tie a double layer of brown paper or newspaper around the outside of the tin to protect the cake during cooking, and place an ovenproof container of water in the oven to help keep your cake moist.

6 Bake for the stated time then reduce the heat to 120°C/250°F/Gas ½ and bake further for the time suggested. When ready the cake will be firm to the touch and a skewer inserted into the centre will come out clean. Allow to cool in the tin.

7 Leaving the lining paper on, wrap the cake in baking parchment then foil. Never store your cake in foil only, as the fruit acid will attack the foil. Store in a cool, dry place.

25.5cm (10in) round	28cm (11in) round	30cm (12in) round	33cm (13in) round	35.5cm (14in) round
23cm (9in) square	25.5cm (10in) square	28cm (11in) square	30cm (12in) square	33cm (13in) square
350g (12oz)	450g (1lb)	550g (1¼lb)	675g (1lb 7oz)	800g (1¾lb)
350g (12oz)	450g (1lb)	550g (1¼lb)	675g (1lb 7oz)	800g (1¾lb)
350g (12oz)	450g (1lb)	550g (1¼lb)	675g (1lb 7oz)	800g (1¾lb)
175g (6oz)	225g (8oz)	275g (10oz)	350g (12oz)	400g (14oz)
45ml (3 tbsp)	60ml (4 tbsp)	75ml (5 tbsp)	90ml (6 tbsp)	105ml (7 tbsp)
350g (12oz)	450g (1lb)	550g (1¼lb)	675g (1lb 7oz)	800g (1¾lb)
75g (3oz)	100g (3½oz)	150g (5oz)	175g (6oz)	200g (7oz)
7.5ml (1½ tsp)	10ml (2 tsp)	12.5ml (2½ tsp)	15ml (1 tbsp)	17.5ml (3½ tsp)
350g (12oz)	450g (1lb)	550g (1¼lb)	675g (1lb 7oz)	800g (1¾lb)
350g (12oz)	450g (1lb)	550g (1¼lb)	675g (1lb 7oz)	800g (1¾lb)
6	8	10	12	14
25ml (1½ tbsp)	30ml (2 tbsp)	37.5ml (2½ tbsp)	45ml (3 tbsp)	52.5ml (3½ tbsp)
3.5ml (¾ tsp)	5ml (1 tsp)	6.5ml (1¼ tsp)	7.5ml (1½ tsp)	7.5ml (1½ tsp)
175g (6oz)	225g (8oz)	275g (10oz)	350g (12oz)	400g (14oz)
75g (3oz)	100g (3½oz)	150g (5oz)	175g (6oz)	200g (7oz)
1½	2	2½	3	3½
2 hours		2½ hours	2¾ hours	3 hours
4 hours		5½ hours	6¼ hours	7 hours
6 hours		8 hours	9 hours	10 hours

Tip
Add extra brandy while the cake is still cooling. Prick the surface with a skewer and spoon some brandy over.

Madeira cake

This is a firm, moist cake that can be flavoured to suit (see below). This cake is ideal for both carving and covering with sugarpaste and will keep for up to two weeks.

Tip

For in-depth tips and discussion on how to bake the perfect Madeira cake visit the Lindy's Cakes blog.

Madeira cake quantities

Cake sizes		Unsalted (sweet) butter	Caster (superfine) sugar	Self-raising (self-rising) flour	Plain (all-purpose) flour	Eggs (large) (US extra large)	Baking times at 160°C/325°F/ Gas 3
10cm (4in) round/ball	7.5cm (3in) square	75g (3oz)	75g (3oz)	75g (3oz)	40g (1½oz)	1½	45 min–1 hour
13cm (5in) round	10cm (4in) square	115g (4oz)	115g (4oz)	115g (4oz)	50g (2oz)	2	45 min–1 hour
15cm (6in) round	13cm (5in) square/ball	175g (6oz)	175g (6oz)	175g (6oz)	75g (3oz)	3	1–1¼ hours
18cm (7in) round	15cm (6in) square	225g (8oz)	225g (8oz)	225g (8oz)	125g (4½oz)	4	1–1¼ hours
20cm (8in) round	18cm (7in) square/ 15cm (6in) ball	350g (12oz)	350g (12oz)	350g (12oz)	175g (6oz)	6	1¼–1½ hours
23cm (9in) round	20cm (8in) square	450g (1lb)	450g (1lb)	450g (1lb)	225g (8oz)	8	1½–1¾ hours
25.5cm (10in) round	23cm (9in) square	500g (1lb 2oz)	500g (1lb 2oz)	500g (1lb 2oz)	250g (9oz)	9	1½–1¾ hours
28cm (11in) round	25.5cm (10in) square	700g (1½lb)	700g (1½lb)	700g (1½lb)	350g (12oz)	12	1¾–2 hours
30cm (12in) round	28cm (11in) square	850g (1lb 14oz)	850g (1lb 14oz)	850g (1lb 14oz)	425g (15oz)	15	2–2¼ hours
33cm (13in) round	30cm (12in) square	1kg (2¼lb)	1kg (2¼lb)	1kg (2¼lb)	500g (1lb 2oz)	18	2¼–2½ hours
35.5cm (14in) round	33cm (13in) square	1.2kg (2lb 10oz)	1.2kg (2lb 10oz)	1.2kg (2lb 10oz)	600g (1lb 5oz)	21	2½–2¾ hours

1 Preheat the oven to 160°C/325°F/Gas 3. Grease and line the cake tin (pan) with baking parchment (see Lining cake tins). To prevent the sides crusting and the top doming, tie a double layer of brown paper or newspaper around the outside or use one of the commercial products now available for this purpose.

2 Cream the butter and sugar in a large mixing bowl until light, fluffy and very pale – I find this takes about five minutes in a mixer. Sift the flours together in a separate bowl.

3 Beat the eggs – they should be at room temperature – into the creamed mixture, one at a time, following each with a spoonful of flour to prevent the mixture curdling. Sift the remaining flour into the creamed mixture and fold in carefully with a large metal spoon. Add the flavouring, if using.

4 Transfer to the lined bakeware and bake for the time stated. You may need to protect the top of your cake while baking to prevent it crusting too much – I usually put a baking sheet on the shelf above my cake throughout the baking process. When the cake is ready it will be well risen, firm to the touch and a skewer inserted into the centre will come out clean.

5 Leave the cake to cool in the tin (pan) then, leaving the lining paper on, wrap the cake in foil or place in an airtight container for at least 12 hours before cutting to allow the cake to settle.

Flavourings

Traditionally, Madeira cake is lemon flavoured, but it can also be made with other flavourings (amounts for a six-egg quantity cake; adjust the amounts for other quantities):

★ **Lemon**: Grated rind of two lemons

★ **Vanilla**: 5ml (1 tsp) vanilla extract

★ **Cherry**: 350g (12oz) glacé (candied) cherries, halved

★ **Fruit**: 350g (12oz) currants, raisins or dates

★ **Coconut**: 110g (3¾oz) desiccated (dry unsweetened shredded) coconut

★ **Almond**: 5ml (1 tsp) almond extract and 45ml (3 tbsp) ground almonds

Baking Mini-Cakes

Mini-cakes are great fun to make and are ideal to give as presents. You can cut your mini-cakes individually from larger cakes or use bakeware (such as a multi mini cake pan) that allows you to bake a number of small cakes at once.

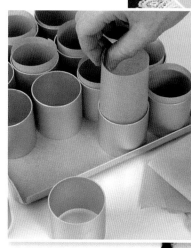

Using specially designed tins

★ Choose a recipe for your mini-cakes – all the cake recipes in this book work well. Line the tins (pans) (see Lining cake tins).

★ Half fill each section of the cake tin with the mixture. I have found the best way of doing this is to pipe the mixture into the tin using a large piping (pastry) bag.

★ Bake the cakes – the time required will very much depend on the type of cake and size of tins but as a guide, 5cm (2in) round sponge mini-cakes usually take 15–20 minutes and 5cm (2in) round fruit cakes take an hour.

★ Leave the cakes to cool in the tin.

Tip
Mini-cakes can dry out quickly so try not to leave them uncovered for any length of time.

Using a Ball Tin

How you bake your cake in a ball tin (pan) depends on the type of cake you are making:

Fruit cake

Pile the mixture into the lower half of the tin, creating a dome, the height of which should be about 1–2cm (⅜–¾in) from the top of the tin when it is assembled. This small space allows the mixture to rise and fill the tin while baking.

Sponge cakes

Bake sponge cake balls in two halves. Allow the halves to cool in the tin then level each cake using the edge of the tin and stick the two halves together with buttercream or chocolate ganache to create a perfect sphere.

Adapting a Favourite Recipe

If you have a favourite recipe that you would like to use to bake a different-sized cake then just refer to the chart below and adapt it accordingly.

How to use the chart

The chart assumes that your own basic recipe will be for a 20cm (8in) round cake, as this is the most common size. Therefore, if you want to make a 25.5cm (10in) round cake, for example, look at the chart and you will see that you need one and a half times the quantity of your usual recipe. If you wish to use a tin (pan) that is not mentioned in the chart, such as a pre-formed shaped tin or oval, fill a 20cm (8in) tin with water and compare it with the quantity of water that your tin holds. The basic recipe quantity can then be multiplied or divided as necessary.

Recipe adaptation chart

Cake sizes			Multiples of your own basic recipe (approximate quantities)
Round	Square	Ball	
7.5cm (3in)			1/8
10cm (4in)	7.5cm (3in)	10cm (4in)	1/4
12.5cm (5in)	10cm (4in)		1/3
15cm (6in)	12.5cm (5in)	13cm (5in)	1/2
18cm (7in)	15cm (6in)		3/4
20cm (8in	18cm (7in)	15cm (6in)	1
23cm (9in)	20cm (8in)		1 1/4
25.5cm (10in)	23cm (9in)		1 1/2
28cm (11in)	25.5cm (10in)		2
30cm (12in)	28cm (11in)		2 1/2
33cm (13in)	30cm (12in)		3
35.5cm (14in)	33cm (13in)		3 1/2

Tip for tiered cakes

★ When making tiered cakes it is very popular to provide different flavours on each tier so that there is something for everyone. However you may need to adjust the sizes you bake slightly. For example, a finished covered fruit cake will be at least 1cm (⅜in) wider than say a chocolate or Madeira cake of the same size due to the additional layer of marzipan. Therefore, when I am baking a mixture of fruit and Madeira, I bake the Madeira cake a size larger and cut it down so that the balance between the sizes is maintained.

Tips for large cakes

★ Baking times will depend on your oven as well as the cake tin (pan) used and the depth of cake.

★ When baking a sponge cake, wrap paper around the outside of the tin as you would a fruit cake to prevent the edges of the cake becoming too dry.

★ Once the crust is formed on the cake, protect it from burning by either placing a paper or foil lid over the cake or placing a baking tray on a shelf in the oven directly above the cake.

★ Check that your oven is large enough to bake the cake – Agas and Rayburns for example will not bake anything larger than 30.5cm (12in) and some tins of this size will not fit.

Tip

For more explanation and discussion about adapting your recipes, visit the Lindy's Cakes blog.

Baking Cupcakes

Baking cupcakes should be fun! First of all choose your cupcake cases and then choose a recipe. The recipes in this book are to help and inspire you, but any cake recipe will work so don't be afraid to experiment with flavours to create something unique to you. Here are just two of my favourite cupcake recipes. Further exciting cupcake recipes can be found in my book *Bake Me I'm Yours … Cupcake Celebration* (D&C, 2010).

Sticky ginger cupcakes

My all-time favourite recipe. I love moist, tasty cakes and this fits the bill superbly – fantastic comfort food! These are best eaten within a week. This recipe also works well as a 13cm (5in) round cake (baking time 1½ hours).

Ingredients *Makes 15–20 depending on case size*
- ☆ 120g (4¼oz) unsalted (sweet) butter
- ☆ 100g (3½oz) dark brown soft sugar (molasses sugar)
- ☆ 60ml (4 tbsp) golden syrup (corn syrup)
- ☆ 60ml (4 tbsp) black treacle (molasses)
- ☆ 150ml (¼ pint) milk
- ☆ 2 eggs, beaten
- ☆ 7.5ml (1½ tsp) vanilla extract
- ☆ 4 pieces of stem ginger, drained from syrup and chopped
- ☆ 230g (8oz) self-raising (self-rising) flour
- ☆ 1½ tbsp ground ginger
- ☆ 5ml (1 tsp) mixed spice

1 Preheat the oven to 170°C/325°F/Gas 3 and line bun or muffin trays with paper cupcake cases.

2 Place the butter, sugar, syrup and treacle (molasses) into a saucepan and warm over a low heat until the sugar has dissolved.

3 Stir in the milk and allow the mixture to cool.

4 When cooled, beat in the eggs, vanilla and stem ginger.

5 Sift the flour and spices into a bowl and make a well in the centre.

6 Gradually pour the cooled liquid into the well and beat with a wooden spoon until combined.

7 Pour or pipe the mixture into the cupcake cases. They should be about three-quarters full.

8 Bake for 20 minutes or until a fine skewer inserted comes out clean.

9 Cool the cupcakes for five minutes before removing them to a wire rack to cool completely.

Tips for successful cupcakes

- ★ Always use only the finest ingredients.
- ★ Accurately measuring your ingredients is vital.
- ★ Bring all your ingredients to room temperature before mixing your cupcake batter.
- ★ Ensure your cupcake pan is thoroughly clean before adding the cases.
- ★ Fill your cases by pouring or piping if the batter is thin or by using a spoon if it is thick.
- ★ Preheat your oven and bake your cupcakes at the correct temperature. Oven thermometers are a useful check.
- ★ If you know your oven heat is uneven, rotate your pan halfway through the baking time.
- ★ Using a fan oven can dry out small cakes quickly, so reduce the temperature stated in each recipe by 10 degrees.
- ★ Cupcakes must be completely cold before you decorate them.
- ★ Undecorated cupcakes can usually be frozen for up to a month.

Orange and poppy seed cupcakes

I fell in love with these delicious cakes on a recent teaching trip to Australia – the tangy flavour and interesting texture of the poppy seeds and orange peel had me hooked! These keep slightly longer than the ginger cakes but are best eaten within two weeks. This recipe also works well as a 13cm (5in) round cake (baking time 1½ hours).

Ingredients *Makes 15–20 depending on case size*
- ☆ 185g (6oz) unsalted (sweet) butter
- ☆ 160g (5oz) caster (superfine) sugar
- ☆ 100g (3½oz) marmalade
- ☆ 1ml (¼ tsp) almond extract
- ☆ Zest of two oranges
- ☆ 80ml (3 fl oz) orange juice
- ☆ 185g (6oz) self-raising (self-rising) flour
- ☆ 60g (2oz) ground almonds
- ☆ 40g (1½oz) poppy seeds
- ☆ 50g (2oz) mixed peel
- ☆ 3 large (US extra large) eggs, lightly beaten

1 Preheat the oven to 170°C/325°F/Gas 3 and line bun or muffin trays with paper cupcake cases.

2 Place the butter, sugar, marmalade, almond essence, orange zest and juice in a pan and stir over a low heat until melted. Allow to cool.

3 Sift the flour, almonds and poppy seeds into a bowl, add the mixed peel then make a well in the centre.

4 Gradually pour the cooled liquid into the well and mix until smooth.

5 Add the eggs and mix until combined.

6 Pour or pipe the mixture into the cupcake cases. They should be about three-quarters full.

7 Bake for 20 minutes or until a fine skewer inserted comes out clean.

8 Cool the cupcakes for five minutes before removing them to a wire rack to cool completely.

9 Brush with orange liquor such as Cointreau before icing.

Experimentation

If you decide to experiment with other recipes, here are some things to bear in mind:

★ Each cake recipe will rise differently; some recipes don't rise at all while others double, so I suggest you make a trial batch filling the cupcake cases at different levels to find the optimum height for your recipe.

★ Typically cupcakes bake for around 20 minutes, but ovens do vary so you should test and retest as necessary.

★ Make a note of the shape of the top of the cupcake; some will be fairly flat while others will be quite domed. The shape can be important when choosing the type of decoration to use.

Tip

Bake an orange cake by omitting the poppy seeds or replace the orange zest and juice with lemon.

Baking Cookies

Fundamental to any decorated cookie is the taste and shape of the cookie itself. When choosing a recipe it's important to opt for one that retains its shape and doesn't spread too much while baking. All the examples in this book can be recreated with either of the recipes below. Follow the tips to create fresh and flavoursome cookies every time.

Vanilla cookies

Ingredients *Makes 15–20 depending on cutter size*
- ✰ 75g (3oz) unsalted (sweet) butter, diced
- ✰ 1 egg, beaten
- ✰ 275g (10oz) plain (all-purpose) flour, sifted
- ✰ 30ml (2 tbsp) golden syrup (corn syrup)
- ✰ 5ml (1 tsp) baking powder
- ✰ 100g (3½oz) caster (superfine) sugar
- ✰ 2.5ml (½ tsp) vanilla extract

1 Preheat the oven to 170ºC/325ºF/Gas 3.

2 Place the dry ingredients into a mixing bowl.

3 Add the butter and rub together with your fingertips until the mixture resembles fine breadcrumbs.

4 Make a hollow in the centre and pour in the beaten egg, syrup and vanilla extract.

5 Mix together well until you have a ball of dough.

6 Place the dough in a plastic bag and chill in the fridge for 30 minutes.

7 Roll the dough out on a lightly floured surface to 5mm (³⁄₁₆in) thick, ideally using spacers, and stamp out the cookies using your chosen cutters. Lightly knead and re-roll the trimmings together again to use up all the dough.

8 Place the cookies on baking sheets and bake for 12–15 minutes, until lightly coloured and firm but not crisp.

9 Leave on the tray for two minutes before transferring to a wire rack to cool completely.

Spiced orange cookies

Ingredients *Makes 15–20 depending on cutter size*
- ✰ 75g (3oz) unsalted (sweet) butter
- ✰ 75g (3oz) soft brown sugar (molasses sugar)
- ✰ 30ml (2 tbsp) honey
- ✰ Zest of one orange
- ✰ 10ml (2 tsp) orange juice
- ✰ 225g (8oz) plain (all-purpose) flour, sifted
- ✰ 5ml (1 tsp) bicarbonate of soda
- ✰ 5ml (1 tsp) cinnamon

1 Preheat the oven to 170ºC/325ºF/Gas 3.

2 Place the butter, sugar, honey, orange zest and juice in a saucepan and heat gently until the sugar has dissolved and the butter has melted.

3 Sieve the flour and dry ingredients in a bowl and add the melted ingredients. Mix well until the dough becomes firm.

4 Place the dough in a plastic bag and chill in the fridge for 40 minutes.

5 Roll the dough out on a lightly floured surface to 5mm (³⁄₁₆in) thick, ideally using spacers, and stamp out the cookies using your chosen cutters. Lightly knead and re-roll the trimmings together again to use up all the dough.

6 Place the cookies on baking sheets and bake for 12–15 minutes, until lightly coloured and firm but not crisp.

7 Leave on the tray for two minutes before transferring to a wire rack to cool completely.

Tips for successful cookies

- ★ Use only the finest and freshest ingredients.
- ★ Use unsalted (sweet) butter – spreadable butters and low-calorie spreads can change the consistency of the dough. Butter gives cookies their flavour and crisp outer texture.
- ★ Mix the dry ingredients thoroughly before adding the liquids.
- ★ Do not over mix the dough, as this will toughen it – just mix until the flour is incorporated.
- ★ Make sure you leave space between the cookies on the baking sheet to allow them to expand a little.
- ★ Try to bake cookies of a similar size in the same batch to avoid over baking smaller cookies.
- ★ Place dough to be baked on cool baking sheets. Rotate baking sheets and rinse and wipe clean between batches.
- ★ Watch the baking time. Always check cookies at the minimum baking time. Even one minute over can mean ruined cookies.
- ★ Cool cookies on wire racks to stop them becoming soggy.
- ★ Make the cookies up to one month in advance and store them un-iced in an airtight container in the freezer.

Sugar Recipes

Most of the sugar recipes used in this book for covering, modelling and decoration can easily be made at home. Use edible paste colours to colour them according to the individual project.

Sugarpaste (rolled fondant)

Used to cover cakes and boards, ready-made sugarpaste can be obtained from major supermarkets and cake-decorating suppliers, and is available in white and the whole colour spectrum. It is also easy and inexpensive to make your own.

Ingredients *Makes 1kg (2¼lb)*
- ☆ 60ml (4 tbsp) cold water
- ☆ 20ml (4 tsp/1 sachet) powdered gelatine
- ☆ 125ml (4 fl oz) liquid glucose
- ☆ 15ml (1 tbsp) glycerine
- ☆ 1kg (2¼lb) icing (confectioners') sugar, sifted, plus extra for dusting

1 Place the water in a small bowl, sprinkle over the gelatine and soak until spongy. Stand the bowl over a saucepan of hot but not boiling water and stir until the gelatine is dissolved. Add the glucose and glycerine, stirring until well blended and runny.

2 Put the sifted icing (confectioners') sugar in a large bowl. Make a well in the centre and slowly pour in the liquid ingredients, stirring constantly. Mix well.

3 Turn out on to a surface dusted with icing (confectioners') sugar and knead until smooth, sprinkling with extra sugar if the paste becomes too sticky. The paste can be used immediately or tightly wrapped and stored in a plastic bag until required.

Modelling paste

Used to add decoration to cakes, this versatile paste keeps its shape well and dries harder than sugarpaste. Although there are commercial pastes available, it is easy and a lot cheaper to make your own – I always do!

Ingredients *Makes 225g (8oz)*
- ☆ 225g (8oz) sugarpaste (rolled fondant)
- ☆ 5ml (1 tsp) gum tragacanth

Make a well in the sugarpaste and add the gum tragacanth. Knead in. Wrap in a plastic bag and allow the gum to work before use. You will begin to feel a difference in the paste after an hour or so, but it is best left overnight. The modelling paste should be firm but pliable with a slight elastic texture. Kneading the modelling paste makes it warm and easy to work with.

★ Modelling paste tips

- ☆ Gum tragacanth is a natural gum available from cake-decorating suppliers.
- ☆ If time is short use CMC (Tylose) instead of gum tragacanth – this a synthetic alternative but it works almost straight away.
- ☆ Placing your modelling paste in a microwave for a few seconds is an excellent way of warming it for use.
- ☆ If you have previously added a large amount of colour to your paste and it is consequently too soft, an extra pinch or two of gum tragacanth will be necessary.
- ☆ If your paste is crumbly or too hard to work, add a touch of white vegetable fat (shortening) and a little cooled boiled water and knead until softened.

Tip

For tips and discussion about making your own sugarpaste, visit the Lindy's Cakes blog.

Buttercream

Buttercream is used as a filling between layers of cake, as a glue to attach sugarpaste to cakes and as a topping on cupcakes.

★ Standard buttercream

Ingredients *Makes 450g (1lb)*
☆ 110g (3¾oz) unsalted (sweet) butter
☆ 350g (12oz) icing (confectioners') sugar
☆ 15–30ml (1–2 tbsp) milk or water
☆ A few drops of vanilla extract or alternative flavouring

1 Place the butter in a bowl and beat until light and fluffy.
2 Sift the icing (confectioners') sugar into the bowl and continue to beat until the mixture changes colour.
3 Add just enough milk or water to give a firm but spreadable consistency.
4 Flavour by adding the vanilla or alternative flavouring, then store the buttercream in an airtight container until required.

★ Swiss meringue buttercream

For me this is the best type of buttercream for cupcakes because it is less sweet and it has a beautiful glossy finish. However be warned, this buttercream is not stable above about 15°C (59°F), so not suitable for hot days or warm climates!

Ingredients *Makes 500g (1lb 1½oz)*
☆ 4 large (US extra large) egg whites
☆ 250g (9oz) caster (superfine) sugar
☆ 250g (9oz) unsalted (sweet) butter, softened
☆ A few drops of vanilla extract

1 Place the egg whites and sugar in a bowl over a saucepan of simmering water. Stir to prevent the egg whites cooking.
2 Once the sugar crystals have dissolved, remove the bowl from the heat and whisk the meringue to its full volume and until the mixture is cool – about five minutes.
3 Add the butter and vanilla and continue to whisk for about 10 minutes. The mixture will reduce in volume and look curdled – don't panic, just keep whisking until the icing has a smooth, light and fluffy texture.
4 This buttercream is stable at a cool room temperature for a day or two. Store any unused buttercream in a refrigerator and re-beat before using.

★ Flavouring buttercream

Try replacing the liquid in the recipes with:
☆ Alcohols such as whisky, rum or brandy
☆ Other liquids such as coffee, melted chocolate, lemon curd or fresh fruit purees
Or add:
☆ Nut butters to make a praline flavour
☆ Flavours such as mint or rose extract

Flower paste

Available commercially from sugarcraft suppliers, flower paste (also known as petal or gum paste) is used to make delicate sugar flowers. It can be bought in white and a variety of colours. There are many varieties available so try a few to see which you prefer. Alternatively, it is possible to make your own, but it is a time-consuming process and you will need a heavy-duty mixer.

Ingredients *Makes 500g (1lb 2oz)*
☆ 500g (1lb 2oz) icing (confectioners') sugar
☆ 15ml (1 tbsp) gum tragacanth
☆ 25ml (1½ tbsp) cold water
☆ 10ml (2 tsp) powered gelatine
☆ 10ml (2 tsp) liquid glucose
☆ 15ml (1 tbsp) white vegetable fat (shortening)
☆ 1 medium egg white

1 Sieve the icing (confectioners') sugar and gum tragacanth into the greased mixing bowl of a heavy-duty mixer (the grease eases the strain on the machine).
2 Place the water in a small bowl, sprinkle over the gelatine and soak until spongy. Stand the bowl over a saucepan of hot but not boiling water and stir until the gelatine is dissolved. Add the glucose and white vegetable fat (shortening) to the gelatine and continue heating until all the ingredients are melted and mixed.
3 Add the glucose mixture and egg white to the icing (confectioners') sugar. Beat the mixture very slowly until mixed – at this stage it will be a beige colour – then increase the speed to maximum until the paste becomes white and stringy.
4 Grease your hands and remove the paste from the bowl. Pull and stretch the paste several times, and then knead together. Place in a plastic bag and store in an airtight container. Leave the paste to mature for at least 12 hours.

★ Flower paste tips

☆ Flower paste dries quickly so when using, cut off only as much as you need and reseal the remainder.
☆ Work it well with your hands – it should 'click' between your fingers when it is ready to use.
☆ If it is too hard and crumbly, add a little egg white and white vegetable fat (shortening) – the fat slows down the drying process and the egg white makes it more pliable.

Pastillage

This paste is used to make sugar pieces that extend above or to the side of a cake and also to make sugarcraft moulds. This is an extremely useful paste because, unlike modelling paste, it sets extremely hard and is not affected by moisture the way other pastes are. However, the paste crusts quickly and is brittle once dry. You can buy it in a powdered form, to which you add water, but it is easy to make yourself.

Ingredients *Makes 350g (12oz)*
- ☆ 1 egg white
- ☆ 300g (11oz) icing (confectioners') sugar, sifted
- ☆ 10ml (2 tsp) gum tragacanth

1 Put the egg white into a large mixing bowl. Gradually add enough icing (confectioners') sugar until the mixture combines together into a ball. Mix in the gum tragacanth and then turn the paste out onto a work board or work surface and knead well.

2 Incorporate the remaining icing (confectioners') sugar into the pastillage to give a stiff paste. Store in a plastic bag placed in an airtight container in a refrigerator for up to one month.

Chocolate ganache

Used as a filling or coating for cakes, I like to use it on cupcakes. A must for all chocoholics – use the best chocolate you can source for a really indulgent topping.

★ Dark chocolate ganache
Ingredients
- ☆ 200g (7oz) dark chocolate
- ☆ 200ml (7 fl oz) double cream

★ White chocolate ganache
Ingredients
- ☆ 600g (1lb 5oz) white chocolate
- ☆ 80ml (2¾ fl oz) double cream

Melt the chocolate and cream together in a bowl over a saucepan of gently simmering water, stirring to combine. Alternatively use a microwave on low power, stirring thoroughly every 20 seconds or so. The ganache can be used warm once it has thickened slightly and is of a pouring consistency or it can be left to cool so that it can be spread with a palette knife. Alternatively, once cooled completely it can be whisked to give a lighter texture.

Royal icing

Use royal icing for stencil work and for piping fine details. Below are recipes for two methods.

★ Quick royal icing

This is a very quick method, which is ideal if time is short or you just wish to just pipe a few details or use a stencil.

Ingredients
- ☆ 1 large (US extra large) egg white
- ☆ 250g (9oz) icing (confectioners') sugar, sifted

Put the egg white in a bowl, lightly beat to break it down then gradually beat in the icing sugar until the icing is glossy and forms soft peaks.

★ Professional royal icing

This is a more involved method that gives you a better quality of icing, ideal for piping finer details. Make sure all your equipment is spotless, as even small residues of grease will affect the icing.

Ingredients
- ☆ 90g (3oz) egg white (approx 3 eggs or equivalent of dried albumen)
- ☆ 455g (1lb) icing (confectioners') sugar, sifted
- ☆ 5–7 drops of lemon juice (if using fresh eggs)

1 Separate the egg whites the day before needed, sieve through a fine sieve or tea strainer, cover and then place in a refrigerator to allow the egg white to strengthen.

2 Place the egg whites into the bowl of a mixer, stir in the icing (confectioners') sugar and add the lemon juice.

3 Using the whisk attachment, beat as slowly as possible for between 10 and 20 minutes until the icing reaches soft peaks. How long it takes will depend on your mixer. Take care not to over mix – test by lifting a little icing out of the bowl. If the icing forms a peak that bends over slightly, it is the correct consistency.

4 Store in an airtight container, cover the top surface with cling film (plastic wrap) and then a clean damp cloth to prevent the icing forming a crust, before adding the lid and placing in a refrigerator.

Tip

For best results bring royal icing back to room temperature before using.

Glues

You can often just use water to stick your sugar decorations to your cakes, however if you find you need something a little stronger here are two options:

★ Sugar glue

This is quick, easy, instant glue to make and is my preferred choice. Break up pieces of white modelling paste into a small container and cover with boiling water. Stir until dissolved or to speed up the process place in a microwave for 10 seconds before stirring. This produces a thick, strong glue, which can be easily thinned by adding some more cooled boiled water. If a stronger glue is required, use pastillage rather than modelling paste as the base, useful for delicate work.

★ Gum glue

Clear gum glue is available commercially, often known as edible glue, but it is very easy and much cheaper to make it yourself. The basic ingredients are I part CMC (Tylose) to 20 parts warm water, which translates into 1.5ml (¼ tsp) CMC (Tylose) to 30ml (2 tbsp) warm water. Place the CMC (Tylose) into a small container with a lid, add the warm water and shake well. Leave in refrigerator overnight. In the morning you will have a thick, clear glue that can be used to stick your sugar work together.

Piping gel

Piping gel is a multi-purpose transparent gel that is excellent for attaching sugarpaste to cookies. It also can add shimmering accents and colourful highlights. It is available commercially but is just as easy to make.

Ingredients
* ☆ 30ml (2 tbsp) powered gelatine
* ☆ 30ml (2 tbsp) cold water
* ☆ 500ml (18 fl oz) golden syrup (corn syrup)

Sprinkle the gelatine over the cold water in a small saucepan and leave to set for about five minutes. Heat on low until the gelatine has become clear and dissolved – do not boil. Add the syrup and stir thoroughly. Cool and store, refrigerated, for up to two months.

White vegetable fat (shortening)

This is a solid white vegetable fat (shortening) that is often known by a brand name: in the UK, Trex or White Flora; in South Africa, Holsum; in Australia, Copha; and in America, Crisco. These products are more or less interchangeable in cake making.

Apricot glaze

This glaze is traditionally used to stick marzipan to fruit cakes. You can also use other jams or jellies, such as apple jelly. Redcurrant jelly is delicious on chocolate cakes when a marzipan covering is used.

Ingredients
* ☆ 115g (4oz) apricot jam
* ☆ 30ml (2 tbsp) water

Place the jam and water in a pan. Heat gently until the jam has melted, and then boil rapidly for 30 seconds. Strain through a sieve if pieces of fruit are present. Use warm.

Covering Cakes and Boards

Follow these techniques to achieve a neat and professional appearance to your cakes, cupcakes, cookies and cake boards. With care and practice, you will soon find that you have a perfectly smooth finish.

Levelling the cake

Making an accurate cake base is an important part of creating your masterpiece. There are two ways to do this, depending on the cake:

Method 1 Place a set square up against the edge of the cake and, with a sharp knife, mark a line around the top of the cake at the required height: 7–7.5cm (2¾–3in). With a large serrated knife cut around the marked line and across the cake to remove the domed crust.

Method 2 Place a cake board into the base of the tin (pan) in which the cake was baked so that when the cake is placed on top, the outer edge of the cake will be level with the tin, and the dome will protrude above. Take a long, sharp knife and cut the dome from the cake, keeping the knife against the tin (**A**). This will ensure the cake is completely level.

A

Filling cakes

It is not necessary to add fillings to the cake recipes used in this book however many people do like their sponge cakes filled with jam and/or buttercream. To add filling, split the cake into a number of horizontal layers and add your choice of filling (**B**).

B

Marzipan and sugarpaste quantities

Cake sizes			Marzipan and sugarpaste quantities – 5mm (³⁄₁₆in) thickness
Round	Square	Ball	
7.5cm (3in)			275g (10oz)
10cm (4in)	7.5cm (3in)	10cm (4in)	350g (12oz)
12.5cm (5in)	10cm (4in)		425g (15oz)
15cm (6in)	12.5cm (5in)	13cm (5in)	500g (1lb 2oz)
18cm (7in)	15cm (6in)		750g (1lb 10oz)
20cm (8in)	18cm (7in)	15cm (6in)	900g (2lb)
23cm (9in)	20cm (8in)		1kg (2¼lb)
25.5cm (10in)	23cm (9in)		1.25kg (2¾lb)
28cm (11in)	25.5cm (10in)		1.5kg (3lb)
30cm (12in)	28cm (11in)		1.75kg (3¾lb)
33cm (13in)	30cm (12in)		2kg (4½lb)
35.5cm (14in)	33cm (13in)		2.25kg (4lb 15oz)

Note: These are the amounts of marzipan and or sugarpaste you will need to cover one cake, if you are covering more than one then you will need less than the amounts for each cake added together, as you will be able to reuse the trimmings.

Freezing cakes

Freezing your cakes allows you not only to bake them well in advance, but also to carve the cakes more easily without the cake crumbling and falling apart. How hard your cake freezes depends on the settings of your freezer so it may be necessary to let your cake defrost slightly before attempting to carve it.

Covering a cake with marzipan

A fruit cake should be covered with marzipan before the sugarpaste covering is applied, to add flavour, to seal in the moisture and to prevent the fruit staining the sugarpaste.

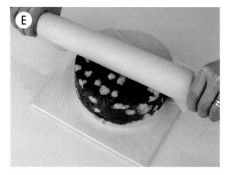

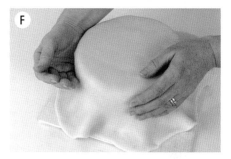

1 Unwrap the cake and roll over the top with a rolling pin to flatten it slightly. If the cake is to sit on a silver-covered cake board, cover the top of the cake with a very thin layer of marzipan and then roll over this with a rolling pin (**C**). (This is to prevent the acid in the fruit dissolving the silver covering of the board, especially important if the cake is going to be kept for any length of time once covered.)

2 Turn the cake over so that the flatter surface (the base) becomes the top and place on a cake board covered in waxed paper. Trim the excess marzipan from the sides.

3 Knead the marzipan so that it becomes supple (see tip below).

4 Brush warm apricot glaze into the gap around the base of the cake. Roll a long sausage of marzipan and place it around the base of the cake, press it under the cake with the help of a smoother, to fill any gaps (**D**).

5 Brush the cake with warm apricot glaze and use small pieces of marzipan to fill any holes in the cake. Roll out the marzipan between 5mm (³⁄₁₆in) spacers, using icing (confectioners') sugar or white vegetable fat (shortening) to stop it sticking to your work board or work surface. Turn the marzipan around while rolling to maintain an appropriate shape, but do not turn the marzipan over.

6 Lift up the marzipan over a rolling pin and place over the cake (**E**). Smooth the top of the cake with a smoother to remove any air bubbles then gently ease the marzipan down the sides of the cake using a cupped hand and an upward motion, opening up any pleats as you go (**F**). Smooth the top curved edge with the palm of your hand and the sides with a smoother.

7 Gradually press down with the smoother around the edge of the cake into the excess marzipan then trim this away to create a neat edge (**G**). Allow the marzipan to harden in a warm, dry place for 24–48 hours to give a firmer base before decorating.

Marzipan tips

★ Choose a white marzipan with a smooth texture and high almond content (at least 23.5 per cent).

★ Don't use icing (confectioners') sugar with added cornflour (cornstarch) to roll out marzipan, as this may cause fermentation.

★ Ensure that nobody who is going to be eating the cake is allergic to nuts – this is very important as nut allergies are serious and can have fatal consequences.

Tip
Do not over knead marzipan as this releases oils and changes its consistency.

Covering a cake with sugarpaste

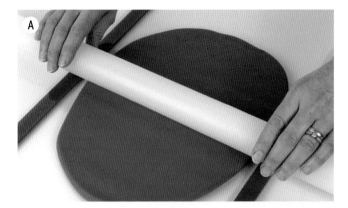

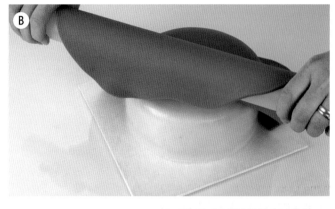

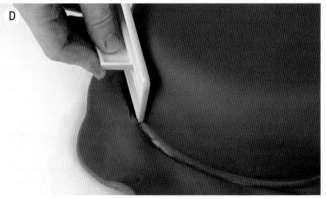

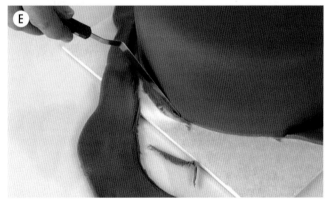

1 For a fruit cake, moisten the surface of the marzipan with an even coating of clear spirit, such as gin or vodka, to prevent air bubbles forming under the sugarpaste. For sponge cakes, place the cake on a hardboard cake board the same size as the cake and place on waxed paper. Cover the cake with a thin layer of buttercream to fill in any holes and help the sugarpaste stick to the surface of the cake.

2 Knead the sugarpaste until warm and pliable. Roll out on a surface lightly smeared with white vegetable fat (shortening) rather than icing (confectioners') sugar – fat works well, and you don't have the problems of icing sugar drying out or marking the sugarpaste. Roll out the paste to a depth of 5mm (³⁄₁₆in) using spacers to ensure an even thickness (**A**).

3 Lift the paste carefully over the top of the cake, supporting it

with a rolling pin, and position it so that it covers the cake (**B**). Using a smoother, smooth the top surface of the cake to remove any lumps and bumps. Smooth the top edge using the palm of your hand. Always make sure your hands are clean and dry with no traces of cake crumbs before smoothing sugarpaste.

4 Using a cupped hand and an upward movement, encourage the sugarpaste on the sides of the cake to adjust to the shape of your cake (**C**). Do not press down on any pleats in the paste, instead open them out and redistribute the paste, until the cake is completely covered. Smooth the sides using a smoother.

5 Take the smoother and while pressing down, run the flat edge around the base of the cake to create a cutting line (**D**). Trim away the excess paste with a palette knife (**E**) to create a neat, smooth edge (**F**).

Covering a cake to give sharp corners

Sometimes, you may wish to have sharp corners on your cake, as seen on the Stacked Hatboxes cake in the Stencilling chapter. To do this you will need to cover the cake with separate pieces of sugarpaste to maintain the edges. This results in a join, so think carefully if it is better to have the join on the side or the top of the cake. For the hatboxes cake the join is on the side, as it is covered by the rim of the lid, so the sides are covered first then the top.

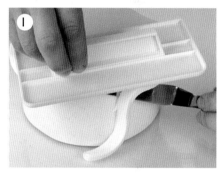

★ The sides

1 Knead the sugarpaste until warm then roll into a long sausage to a length equal to the circumference of the cake. Place the sausage on your work surface and roll over to widen the paste to at least the height of the cake and thin to a thickness of 5mm (³⁄₁₆in). Cut one edge straight.

2 Cover the sides of the cake with a thin layer of buttercream. Carefully roll up the sugarpaste like a bandage then unroll it around the sides of the cake so the cut edge is flush with the lower edge of the cake (**G**). Take a smoother and smooth the paste to give it an even surface.

3 Roughly cut away the excess paste with scissors. Note: you are just removing the excess weight, not giving a neat finish.

4 Place the smoother onto the surface of the sugarpaste so that it partially rests above the edge of the cake then, using a palette knife, neatly remove the excess paste by cutting away from the cake onto the smoother (**H**).

★ The top

1 Roll out some more sugarpaste and use to cover the top of the cake. Roughly cut away the excess overhanging paste with a pair of scissors.

2 Place the smoother onto the surface of the sugarpaste so that it slightly overhangs the edge of the cake then using a palette knife, neatly remove the excess paste by cutting away from the cake onto the smoother (**I**).

Covering a ball cake

1 Place the cake on waxed paper and cover with buttercream or marzipan.

2 Roll out the sugarpaste to a thickness of 5mm (³⁄₁₆in), ideally into a circle the same diameter as the circumference of your cake. Place the paste over the ball cake (**J**), ease the paste around the base of the cake and pull up the excess to form two or more pleats (**K**). Cut the pleats away with scissors and smooth the joins closed (**L**), they should disappear quite readily with the heat of your hand.

3 Trim any excess paste away from the base of the cake. Using a smoother followed by your hand, smooth the surface of the cake with vertical strokes (**M**). It is worth spending time doing this, the paste will not dry out if you continually work it. Set the cake aside to dry.

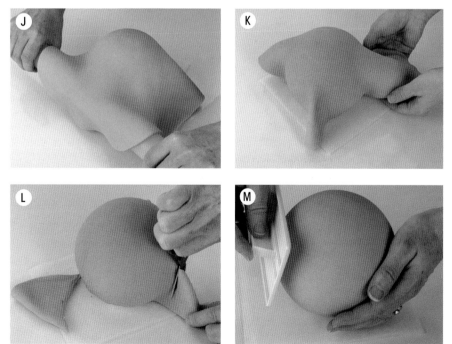

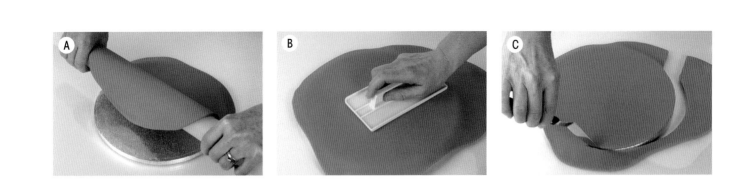

Covering boards

Covering a board with sugarpaste gives you a canvas on which to add decoration to complement and enhance your cake design.

1 Roll out the sugarpaste to a thickness of 4mm (⅛in) or 5mm (³⁄₁₆in) using spacers.

2 Moisten the board with cooled boiled water or sugar glue. Lift up the paste and drape over the board (**A**). Circle a smoother over the paste to achieve a smooth, flat finish to the board (**B**).

3 Cut the paste flush with the sides of the board using a cranked handled palette knife, taking care to keep the edge vertical (**C**). The covered board should ideally be left overnight to dry thoroughly.

Covering the board and its sides

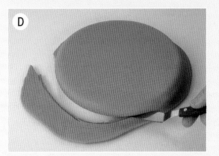

To cover a cake board plus its sides, as seen on the Coral Creation cake in the Piping chapter, firstly place the cake board on a smaller board to lift it off your work surface. Roll out some sugarpaste and place it over the board. Take a smoother and using a circular motion smooth the paste to give a level surface, smooth the curved edge using the palm of your hand. Using a cranked handled palette knife, trim the sugarpaste flush with the underside of the board, taking care to keep the cut horizontal (**D**). Set aside to dry.

Covering mini-cakes

Mini-cakes are covered in exactly the same way as standard cakes, it is just the scale that is different. You will find that the icing pleats more readily so remember to keep opening the pleats (**E**) before smoothing to shape (**F**). You may also find that the sugarpaste is thicker at the bottom of the cake than the top – to help overcome this problem, rotate the cake between to two flat-edged smoothers to help redistribute the paste and ensure the sides of the cake are vertical (**G**).

Tip
If you have air bubbles under the icing, insert a scriber or clean glass-headed dressmakers' pin at an angle and press out the air.

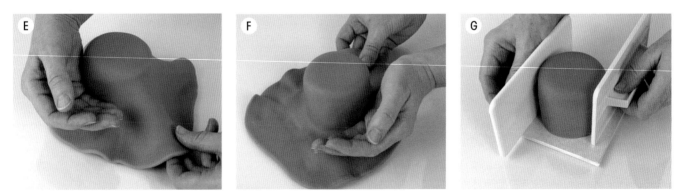

Covering cupcakes

It is worth doing a little preparation before covering your cupcakes. Not all cupcakes come out of the oven perfect, some may need a little trimming with a sharp knife while others benefit from a little building up with an appropriate icing.

1 Check each of your cupcakes to ensure that the decoration is going to sit just as you want it to and remedy any that aren't quite right.

2 The sugarpaste may need a little help to secure it to the cupcakes, so brush the cakes with an appropriate syrup or alcohol or add a thin layer of buttercream or ganache, this also adds flavour and interest to the cakes.

3 Knead the sugarpaste until warm and pliable. Roll out on a surface lightly smeared with white vegetable fat (shortening), rather than icing (confectioners') sugar. Roll out the paste to a depth of 5mm (³⁄₁₆in). It is a good idea to use spacers for this, as they ensure an even thickness (**H**).

4 Cut out circles of sugarpaste using an appropriately sized cutter (**I**). The size of the circle required will be dependant on the cupcake pan and case used and the amount the cakes have domed.

5 Using a palette knife, carefully lift the paste circles onto each cupcake (**J**). Use the palm of your hand to shape the paste to the cupcake, easing the fullness in if necessary.

Covering cookies

Sugarpaste is an excellent and very versatile medium for cookie decoration as it allows you to be extremely creative.

1 Smear white vegetable fat (shortening) over your work surface to prevent the icing sticking. Knead the sugarpaste to warm before use.

2 Roll out the kneaded sugarpaste to a thickness of 5mm (³⁄₁₆in) and cut out a shape using the same cookie cutter used to create the cookie (**K**). Remove the excess paste.

3 Paint piping gel over the top of the baked cookie to act as glue (**L**). Alternatively use buttercream or boiled jam. Carefully lift the sugarpaste shape using a palette knife to prevent distorting the shape and place on top of the cookie (**M**). If the cookie cutter has left a ragged edge around the base of the shape, just carefully tuck this under with a finger before placing on the cookie.

4 Run a finger around the top cut edge of the sugarpaste to smooth and curve it.

Tip
If you are covering only part of a cookie, apply piping gel to that section only.

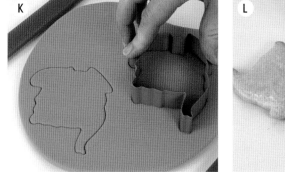

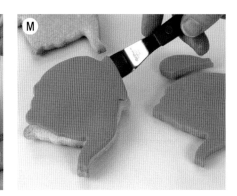

Stacking Cakes

A multi-tiered cake, like a building, needs a structure hidden within it to prevent it from collapsing. It is important that this structure is 'built' correctly to take the loads put upon it, so follow these instructions carefully, as it is worth the time involved to get this stage correct.

Dowelling the cakes

All but the top tier will usually need dowelling to provide support.

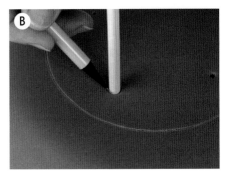

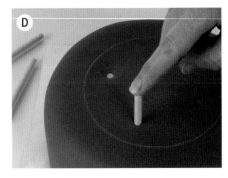

1 Place the cakes to be stacked on hardboard cake boards of the same size as the cakes and cover each cake with sugarpaste, this ensures the boards are not visible yet gives the stacked cakes stability.

2 To support the cakes, dowels need to be inserted into all but the top tier. To do this, take the base cake and place a cake board the same size as the tier above in the centre of the cake. Scribe around the edge of the board to leave a visible outline (**A**).

3 Insert a dowel 2.5cm (1in) in from the scribed line vertically down through the cake to the cake board below. Make a knife scratch or pencil mark on the dowel to mark the exact height (**B**) and remove the dowel.

4 Tape four dowels together. Then, using the mark on the inserted dowel, draw a pencil cutting line over the tape on the four dowels, making sure that the line is 90 degrees to the dowels (a set square helps) (**C**). Next, using a small saw, such as a mitre saw that holds the dowels firm as it cuts, saw across the dowels.

5 Place one of the dowels back in the measuring hole and insert the other dowels vertically down to the cake board at 3, 6 and 9 o'clock to the first one (**D**).

6 Repeat steps 1–5 for all but the top cake. It is essential that all the dowels are inserted vertically, are all the same length and have flat tops.

Dowelling wonky cakes

The only difference when dowelling wonky cakes is that each dowel position will need to be measured and that the tops of the dowels will need to be cut at the same angle as the cake so they will be flush with the icing. I use a ratcheted pipe cutter to do this.

Stacking the cakes

Cover and dowel each cake before stacking. Place 15ml (1 tbsp) royal icing within the scribed area of the base cake and stack the next sized cake on top using the scribed line as a placement guide. Repeat the process with the remaining cakes.

Storage

The following conditions will affect your decorated cakes and cookies. It is therefore best to protect them as much as possible.

☆ Sunlight will fade and alter the colours of icing, so always store in a dark place.

☆ Humidity can have a disastrous effect on modelling paste and pastillage decorations, causing the icing to become soft and to droop if free standing. It can also causes dark colours to bleed into lighter colours and silver decorations, whether edible or not, to tarnish.

☆ Heat can melt icing, especially buttercream, and can prevent the sugarpaste crusting over.

★ Cupcakes

Store cooled cupcakes in an airtight container at room temperature until you are ready to decorate them. Decorate your cakes as close as possible to when they will be eaten to help prevent the cakes drying out. If this is not possible, use foil or high-quality greaseproof cases and cover the whole of the top of each cake to help seal in the moisture.

Cardboard cupcake boxes are the best way to transport cupcakes – they are simply boxes with an insert, which prevents the cakes from sliding. You can stack the boxes so the cupcakes are easy to carry. Boxes are available for the different case sizes and range from single-hole boxes to at least 24 holes.

★ Cakes

Protect your cake by placing it in a clean, covered cardboard cake box, and store somewhere cool and dry, but never in a refrigerator. If the box is slightly larger than the cake and the cake is to be transported, use non-slip matting to prevent the cake moving.

★ Cookies

Cookies keep remarkably well, so you can bake and decorate them well in advance. Once decorated and dried, I like to place my cookies in cookie bags to protect them. However if you have lots to store, allow all the icing and decoration to dry and then store in airtight containers, layering them with kitchen paper.

★ Mini-cakes

A nice way to protect your mini-cakes is to pop them into little PVC cubes, this way they can be displayed and stacked at the same time.

Cake Portions

The number of portions you can get from a cake depends on whether it cuts cleanly and the dexterity of the person cutting it. The fruit cake portions on the chart, right, are based on 2.5cm (1in) square slices but many caterers cut smaller than this. It is always better to overestimate the number of portions required. Sponge cakes are served in 5 x 2.5cm (2 x 1in) portions at least double the size of fruit cake slices. Allow extra cake if you want larger portions for, say, a teatime birthday cake.

★ How to cut a cake

Cut across the centre first then cut parallel lines 2.5cm (1in) apart. Next cut a perpendicular line through the centre, followed by parallel lines of the required width – 5cm (2in) for sponge cake and 2.5cm (1in) for fruit cake.

Portion guide

Cake sizes			Approximate portions	
Round	Square	Ball	Fruit cake 2.5cm (1in) slices	Sponge cake 5 x 2.5cm (2 x 1in) slices
7.5cm (3in)			9	4
10cm (4in)	7.5cm (3in)	10cm (4in)	12	6
12.5cm (5in)	10cm (4in)		16	8
15cm (6in)	12.5cm (5in)	13cm (5in)	24	12
18cm (7in)	15cm (6in)		34	17
20cm (8in)	18cm (7in)	15cm (6in)	46	24
23cm (9in)	20cm (8in)		58	28
25.5cm (10in)	23cm (9in)		70	35
28cm (11in)	25.5cm (10in)		95	47
30cm (12in)	28cm (11in)		115	57
33cm (13in)	30.5cm (12in)		137	68
35.5cm (14in)	33cm (13in)		150	75

Carving

Having a cake of the correct shape is fundamental to any good cake design. If you shy away from carving you are limiting yourself to basic shapes, yet armed with a sharp knife and a little bit of courage it is perfectly possible to sculpt a shape that can turn the ordinary into the extraordinary. Once you have mastered the basics of carving cakes, with a little practice most shapes will be within your grasp. This chapter shows you how to carve a simple shape, how to use templates to create a more complex shape and finally how to create a dramatic wonky cake.

Chapter Contents:

Choosing the Right Cake

★ To fill or not to fill?

★ Tips for carving cakes

Carving a Simple Shape

Using Templates

Carving Wonky Cakes

★ Baking the cakes

★ Carving the top of the base cake

★ Carving the sides of the base cake

★ Carving the upper tiers

★ Adjusting and stacking the cakes

Tip
Be brave when carving, as cakes are not scary and all mistakes are edible!

Modern Masterpiece
The lines of this cake are created by carving each of the tiers at opposing angles to give a quirky wonky effect – perfect for the Kandinsky-inspired design used on it. See the Projects chapter for step-by-step instructions for all the cakes featured in this chapter.

Choosing the Right Cake

It is very important when attempting to carve a cake that you choose a recipe that is dense enough to carve successfully. I tend to use flavoured Madeira or a good-quality chocolate cake (see Baking Cakes), but other recipes work just as well, so do experiment with your favourites. However do not attempt a carved cake with a lovely light fluffy sponge – it will, of course, taste delicious but will be very difficult to carve and may well collapse with the weight of the sugarpaste once covered.

To fill or not to fill?

It is not necessary to add fillings to the cake recipes used in this book. However I have found that many people do like their cakes filled with jam and/or flavoured buttercream. To add a filling, split the cake into a number of horizontal layers and add your choice of filling. For best results when carving, add only thin layers of filling – thick layers tend to make the cake unstable and so less suitable for carving. Also do not be tempted to put jam and buttercream on the same layer as this will cause the top layer to slide, making the cake unsteady.

Tips for carving cakes

★ Use a large, sharp pastry knife when carving. If you use a blunt knife, it can be hard work and the cuts you make may not come away cleanly. You may also find that sections of cake fall away as you carve, which although they can be repaired, is not ideal.

★ It is much easier to carve a frozen cake than a fresh cake. Freezing allows you to bake the cakes in advance and to carve more intricate shapes without the cake crumbling. It may be necessary to let your cake defrost slightly before carving it.

★ How accurately you need to carve depends on the shape. With 'organic' shapes it doesn't matter if it's not completely symmetrical, but for a wonky cake you need to be more exact. Make sure you have a ruler and a set square that starts with zero in the corner, not one with a gap before the measurements start.

Carving a Simple Shape

The following sequence shows you how to carve a heart-shaped cake from a round cake but the principles apply equally to square cakes and other carved shapes.

Patchwork Heart
A heart-shaped cake really shows that you care.

1 Bake a round cake and once cool, level the top. Take a circle of paper the same size as the cake and fold it in half. Draw half of a heart, filling as much or as little of the circle as desired. You will have more cake if you draw a 'chubby' heart and less if you draw a slim, elegant heart. Cut out the folded paper shape using scissors.

2 Place the template on the cake using cocktail sticks (toothpicks) to secure it. Take a sharp knife and cut vertically down through the cake to give your cake a heart outline.

3 Now shape the cake by carefully cutting from the centre down towards the point to form the tip of the heart. Next carve away the sides of the cake by cutting a gentle curve from the centre of the cake down to all the lower edges. Finally, round all the top edges of the heart.

Using Templates

Making templates to carve shapes is often the best way to start. The following sequence shows you how to carve a handbag shape but the same principles can be applied to other shapes.

Fuchsia Fashionista
With a template to guide you, even complicated shapes are possible.

1 Photograph an object from the back, front, side and overhead, making sure the images are as straight as possible rather than being at an angle to the camera. Resize the photographs to create a suitable cake size making sure the height, width and depth dimensions of your images match. Use these images to create templates.

2 Level a square cake and cut it in half. Stack the resulting halves to create a 15cm (6in) deep cake. Cut out two of the front templates. Attach one template to either side of your stacked cake using cocktail sticks (toothpicks).

3 Take a large sharp knife and, holding it at right angles to the templates, carve away the excess cake – this gives you the basic handbag outline.

4 Place the overhead template on top of the carved cake and using this as a guide, curve all the corners of the bag using long straight vertical strokes.

5 Remove the templates then mark the central line on the top of the bag where the clasp will be. Using the side template as a guide to the width, mark a line either side of the central line. Cut into the cake along the marked lines to a depth of approximately 1.5cm (½in). Then holding the knife horizontally, cut from the edge of the cake to the vertical cuts just made.

6 Carving the remainder of the cake has to be done freehand. Remove a little cake at a time from the front and back of the bag until you have a curved, shapely bag. The more you take away from the top of the bag the more slender the bag will look.

7 To shape the sides of the bag, use a small, sharp paring knife. Make a vertical cut at both ends of the clasp section. Then keeping the point of the knife in the cake, cut out a teardrop-shaped wedge of cake from each end. Try and keep the edges of the bag as sharp as possible. Finally round the area below the removed teardrops.

Carving Wonky Cakes

A stacked cake cut at angles is the ultimate challenge for many. However, it is not as difficult as it may seem, as long as you carve the cake one step at a time closely following the step-by-step instructions and check and re-check your carved shapes as you proceed.

Baking the cakes

You will need between two and four round 7.5cm (3in) deep cakes depending on how many tiers you wish to carve. To give your cake a similar look to mine, the difference in size between each cake should be 7.5cm (3in).

Gaudi's Grandeur
The fun and funky shape of this cake – inspired by the work of Antoni Gaudi – may seem tricky but it is easier than you might think.

Carving the top of the base cake

1 Level the base cake to 7.5cm (3in) (if your cake is not this high the result will not look the same as mine and you may need to adjust the measurements. Alternatively, add cake boards under the cake to give extra height). Take four cocktail sticks (toothpicks) and insert one into the top edge of the cake at 45 degrees (12 o'clock). Insert the next opposite the first (6 o'clock) horizontally down the side of the cake, 4–5cm (1½–2in) from the base – heights vary depending on cake size, see chart opposite.

2 Insert two more cocktail sticks (toothpicks) at the midway points between the first two (3 and 9 o'clock) at the height indicated in the chart. You are aiming to create a cutting guide to help carve away the top. Take a long-bladed carving knife and using the cocktail sticks (toothpicks) to guide you, slice through the top of the cake.

3 Leave the slice in place and position a cake board slightly larger than the cake on top. Invert the whole cake, and then remove the main cake section from the top placing it back on its base.

4 Check that the sides are the same height at the same point and adjust as necessary. Spread buttercream (if using a sponge cake) or boiled jam (if using a fruit cake) over the sloping top of the main cake.

5 Slide the top section from its board onto the prepared surface so that the two highest and two lowest sides match thus increasing the angle of the slope. It is now ideal, although not essential if you are in a rush, to freeze the cakes. It is much easier to carve and adjust the shape of wonky cakes when they are frozen.

Carving the sides of the base cake

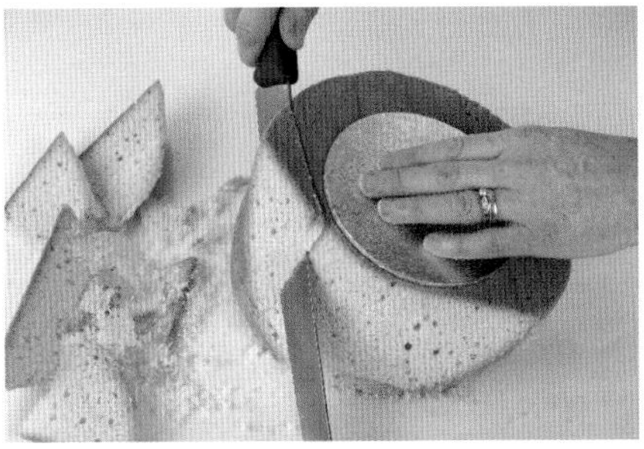

1 Turn the base cake over so it rests on its sloping top. Take a round board of the correct size (see base diameter column of chart) and place it in the centre. Make a shallow cut around the board to mark its position (so it is easy to replace if it slips). Next, carve in small cuts from the edge of the board down to the outside edge of the cake on your work surface.

2 Turn the cake back over and straighten the cut of the sides if necessary. Also check that the cake is symmetrical and adjust as required. If using a sponge cake, take a small knife or a pair of scissors and carefully curve the top edge to complete.

Tip

Take your time getting the fundamental shape of these cakes correct – don't rush, especially if this is your first attempt.

Carving the upper tiers

The only difference when carving the upper tiers of a wonky cake is that the board is not placed centrally on the base. The board needs to be nearer to the highest point of the cake to achieve the best effect, e.g. for a 12.5cm (5in) cake the board should be positioned 1cm (⅜in) from the highest point. See chart below.

Adjusting and stacking the cakes

Stack your cakes, as for the finished cake, to check the side and slope angles – then un-stack and adjust as required with a small sharp knife. When everything is correct, cover, dowel and stack the cakes (see Covering Cakes and Stacking Cakes) ready for decorating.

Wonky cake carving guide for 7.5cm (3in) deep cakes

Size of cake	Heights of sides: Highest point (12 o'clock)	Heights of sides: Lowest point (6 o'clock)	Heights of sides: Midway points (3 & 9 o'clock)	Base diameter	Increase the cake height by adding cake drums to the base, after carving	Upper tiers – position of the board from the highest point
33cm (13in)	7.5cm (3in)	3.75cm (1½in)	5.6cm (2¼in)	28cm (11in)	2 x 15mm (½in) deep cake drum	N/A
30.5cm (12in)	7.5cm (3in)	3.75cm (1½in)	5.6cm (2¼in)	25.5cm (10in)	2 x 15mm (½in) deep cake drum	N/A
28cm (11in)	7.5cm (3in)	4cm (1⅝in)	5.75cm (2¼in)	23cm (9in)	1 x 15mm (½in) deep cake drum	N/A
25.5cm (10in)	7.5cm (3in)	4cm (1⅝in)	5.75cm (2¼in)	20cm (8in)	1 x 15mm (½in) deep cake drum	1.5cm (9/16in)
23cm (9in)	7.5cm (3in)	4.25cm (1⅝in)	5.9cm (2 5/16in)	18cm (7in)	N/A	1.5cm (9/16in)
20cm (8in)	7.5cm (3in)	4.5cm (1¾in)	6cm (2⅜in)	15cm (6in)	N/A	1.25cm (½in)
18cm (7in)	7.5cm (3in)	4.5cm (1¾in)	6cm (2⅜in)	12.5cm (5in)	N/A	1.25cm (½in)
15cm (6in)	7.5cm (3in)	4.75cm (1¾in)	6cm (2⅜in)	10cm (4in)	N/A	1.25cm (½in)
12.5cm (5in)	7.5cm (3in)	5cm (2in)	6.25cm (2½in)	9cm (3½in)	N/A	1cm (⅜in)
10cm (4in)	7.5cm (3in)	5cm (2in)	6.25cm (2½in)	7.5cm (3in)	N/A	8mm (5/16in)
7.5cm (3in)*	7.5cm (3in)	5cm (2in)	6.25cm (2½in)	6cm (2⅜in)	N/A	6mm (¼in)

*7.5cm (3in) cakes are only 7.5cm (3in) high so are not flipped

Colour

One of the most important aspects of decorating a cake is the colours you choose, and getting this absolutely right is something well worth taking your time over. Colour is very subjective but we are all drawn to particular colours. A colour wheel is good starting point when it comes to choosing colours that will work well together. This chapter will give you some ideas for using colour, as well as showing you how to colour your own paste and ways of creating exciting coloured patterns.

Chapter Contents:

Introducing Colour

★ The colour wheel

★ Choosing a colour scheme

★ Colour temperature – warm and cold colours

Food Colourings

Colouring Sugarpaste and Modelling Paste

★ Colour variables

Marbling Patterns

Simple Repeat Patterns

Stripe and Check Patterns

Millefiori Patterns

Tip

Colour combinations go in and out of fashion so try to keep abreast of what's in style in the current season.

Patchwork Heart

The patchwork theme of this cake requires careful balancing of colours and patterns. See the Projects chapter for step-by-step instructions for this cake, plus the materials lists and instructions for all the other cakes and cookies shown in this chapter.

Introducing Colour

When choosing and mixing colours to be used on cakes, a basic knowledge of the theory of colour and its application is particularly useful. The subject of colour is a vast and fascinating one, but these simple guidelines should help you to create successful colour schemes for your cakes.

The colour wheel

This is a system used by artists. The colours of the spectrum are turned into a circle, which reflects the natural order of the colours. A 12-colour division circle consists of the three primary colours (red, blue and yellow, which cannot be made by mixing), three secondary colours (mixtures of two primaries in equal quantities) and six tertiaries (made by mixing primaries and secondaries together e.g. orange mixed with yellow gives yellow-orange).

It is very helpful, at least once, to paint a colour wheel, as it is a very revealing exercise. You will find that although the primaries, in theory, should produce all the other colours, the reality is slightly different – for example different blues are needed to mix green and violet.

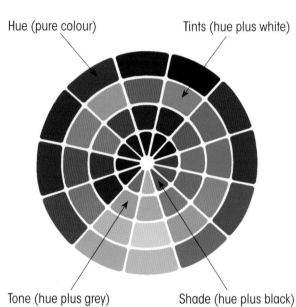

Hue (pure colour)   Tints (hue plus white)

Tone (hue plus grey)   Shade (hue plus black)

Choosing a colour scheme

There are no right or wrong colour combinations but the following are tried-and-tested schemes that make good starting points from which to experiment.

☆ **Monochromatic:** Uses tints, tones and shades of one colour.
☆ **Adjacent:** This uses two, three or four colours lying next to each other on the colour wheel. This combination produces an easy and pleasing harmony as the colours are closely related
☆ **Complementary:** Where the colours lie opposite or approximately opposite on the colour wheel. This works as each pair of colours gives a balance of cool and warm colours, e.g. blue and orange, yellow and violet, and red and green.
☆ **Triadic:** This scheme uses three colours equidistantly spaced on the colour wheel.
☆ **Polychromatic:** The use of many colours together, this often works well using tints, as they are soft colours.

When looking for inspiration for a colour scheme also try looking at the colours used around you, colours used by others in art, on everyday objects, in magazines, on greetings cards and in the folk art of other cultures such as Mexican or African to see what combinations appeal to you. Another idea is to try experimenting with paint sample cards, available from DIY stores.

Colour temperature – warm and cold colours

Orange and red are warm colours whereas blue and green are cold. There are however cooler and warmer versions of every colour. For example, a red mixed with a lot of blue is a cooler colour than a red-orange. It is also interesting that a warm colour appears more intense when placed against a cool colour than if it is placed against another warm or neutral colour.

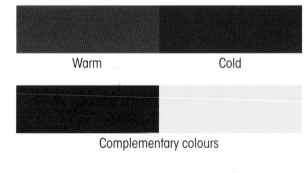

Warm   Cold

Complementary colours

Monochromatic tints

Food Colourings

There are many different edible colouring products available. The ones you need will depend on the type of icing and the effect you wish to achieve.

★ Paste colours

These are concentrated edible colours that are suitable to colour all forms of icing. They can also be diluted with clear alcohol and used as a paint.

★ Liquid colours

A less concentrated form of edible colouring used to colour royal icing or used as a paint. The advantage of using liquid colours for royal icing is that they contain no glycerol, which can prevent royal icing drying.

★ Powder colours

Also known as petal dusts or blossom tints, these are generally used dry and dusted onto the surface of icing, although they can also be mixed into icing to colour it or diluted with alcohol as paint.

★ Lustre colours

These are also an edible dust but with an added shimmer. Use dry or diluted. They work extremely well with stencils.

★ Non-toxic craft dusts and glitters ⚠

Beware, some craft dusts (which tend to be brighter and stronger than food-grade dusts) were originally classified as edible colours but due to changes in international food regulations they are no longer. Therefore these dusts should be used only for display items that will not be consumed. The same is true for non-toxic glitters. Always read the label – if products are edible there will be a best before date and a list of ingredients.

Colouring Sugarpaste and Modelling Paste

Sugarpaste (rolled fondant) and modelling paste are now available commercially in all kinds of colours. However, if you can't find the exact colour you're searching for, or if only a small amount of a colour is required, it is often best to colour your own paste or adjust the colour of a commercial one.

1 Depending on the amount of paste you wish to colour and the depth of colour required, place a little edible paste colour, not liquid colour, on the end of a cocktail stick (toothpick) or a larger amount on the end of a palette knife. Add to the paste.

2 Knead thoroughly, adding more until the desired result is achieved. Be careful with pale colours, as only a little colour is needed. Deep colours, on the other hand, require plenty and will become quite sticky. To overcome this, add a pinch of gum tragacanth and leave for an hour or two; the gum will make the paste firmer and easier to handle. Note: the coloured paste will appear slightly darker when dry.

Tip

It is easier to colour a small amount of paste darker than you need and gradually add this into a larger amount than trying to colour the paste all in one go.

Colour variables

Some variables can affect the colours that you mix – these include the following:

☆ **Time**: Colours often darken over time so if possible leave your paste to rest for a few hours before using, this way you won't have to add as much colour.

☆ **Ingredients**: White vegetable fat (shortening), margarine and butter all make colours turn darker. Lemon juice on the other hand softens colours.

☆ **Light**: Some colours, especially pinks, purple and blues fade in bright light so protect your paste as you work, and your finished creations.

Marbling Patterns

This technique makes the surface of the paste resemble the patterns found in natural marble. Each time you make marbled paste the effect will be different, even if you use the same colours. Use similar colours for a subtle effect or contrasting colours for something more striking.

Tip

Experiment with small amounts of paste to see what colour combinations you like before you commit to colouring large amounts.

1 Choose two or more colours to use (I often use about six different but similar colours) and knead to warm. Break the coloured pastes into small pieces and scatter over your work surface to mix up the colours.

2 Gather the scattered pieces together into a ball and briefly knead together. Cut across the ball to reveal the marbled pattern inside.

3 Place the two half balls next to one another and then roll the paste out between 5mm (³⁄₁₆in) spacers using white vegetable fat (shortening) to prevent sticking. The direction in which you roll the paste will affect the resulting pattern, so try altering the direction you are rolling as the pattern develops.

Distortion If the pattern is not quite as you wish, it is possible to tweak it by stroking the pattern in the paste with a finger to distort it. It is important to do this before the paste has been thinned to 5mm (³⁄₁₆in). Once the pattern has been modified, continue to roll until the paste is an even thickness again.

Butterfly Buttons Bag
Marbling the sugarpaste gives a very pretty, subtle effect to the decoration on this cookie.

Simple Repeat Patterns

Very effective patterned paste can be achieved by rolling shapes of one colour into a different background colour. In the example below, I have used circles to create polka-dot pastes but try it with other shapes, such as flowers, teardrops, stars, hearts and so on. I have chosen to use tones of pink, however you can be more adventurous and use a number of different colours on one background colour.

Dotty Spotty
This repeating pattern is simple to create using the steps here.

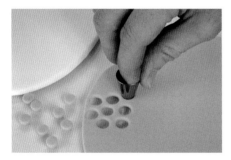

1 Roll out the background paste slightly thicker than 5mm (³⁄₁₆in). Roll out the contrasting colour, fairly thinly, and cut out shapes using an appropriate cutter.

2 Place the shapes either uniformly or randomly over the rolled-out background paste, noting that the pattern will enlarge slightly so you may wish to put your shapes closer together than you require for your finished paste.

3 Roll over the sugarpaste until the paste is 5mm (³⁄₁₆in) thick. The direction in which you roll will elongate your cut out shapes so if you wish to retain the original proportions, roll over your paste in all directions. Interesting shapes can be created, however, if you do just roll in one direction, for example you can turn a circle into an oval, or a rounded heart into an elegant thin one.

Using modelling paste

When using modelling paste, roll out your paste to 1.5mm (¹⁄₁₆in) thick, add your cut out shapes but rather than rolling over the paste, use a smoother to press down firmly on the paste. This helps to blend the pastes without distorting the shapes. If you deliberately want to distort the shapes then use a rolling pin as before.

Tip
Use a stay-fresh mat or a plastic bag to help prevent your rolled-out icing drying out.

Stripe and Check Patterns

Striking geometric patterns can be easily created using this layering technique. Ideally use modelling paste, as it is easier to ensure the lines remain parallel and that the stripes are nice and thin. For a chunkier look, however, use sugarpaste. Use a very sharp knife for this technique – if you don't the stripes will merge together and the clean lines will be lost.

Bring Out the Bunting
Stripes and checks are used to wonderful effect on the bunting and border adorning this mini-cake.

Stripes

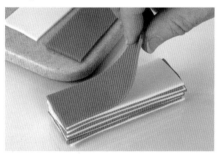

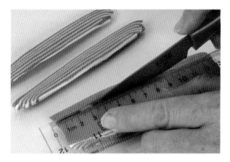

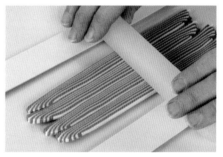

1 Very thinly roll out two colours of paste – the thinner you roll your paste, the thinner the stripes. Cut out similar sized rectangles, smear with a little moisture to make them tacky, and stack in alternating colours. Roll across the top of the pile to secure and thin the paste a little.

2 Place a ruler lengthways on top of the stack and using a sharp knife or craft knife, cut through the stack to create a straight edge. Then repeat at 3mm (⅛in) intervals to create strips. Place the strips under plastic or a stay-fresh mat to prevent them drying out.

3 Take a few strips and place them side by side between narrow spacers and roll along the strips to lengthen and thin the paste. If you wish to widen the stripes, roll across the strips instead. Cut out shapes from this paste as required.

Checks

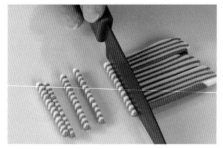

Tip
Work cleanly by wiping your board, tools and cutters when changing colours so you don't end up with discoloured paste.

1 Follow steps 1 and 2 above to create 3mm (⅛in) layers of stripes. Then cut across the stripes to make fingers of tiny squares.

2 Carefully pick up these fingers of paste and place them next to each other to form a checked pattern, they should be moist enough to stick to themselves but if not you can always rub a little moisture onto the cut edges. Carefully roll over the paste with a rolling pin, taking care to maintain the square shapes by rolling in both directions. Cut shapes from the paste as required.

Millefiori Patterns

The term *millefiori* ('a thousand flowers') comes from a glasswork technique that produces distinctive decorative patterns. The patterns are not difficult to create but it does take a little patience. This is an excellent technique for creating animal prints, as can be seen on the Patchwork Heart cake at the start of the chapter.

Millefiori Mug
Modelling paste was used to create the dainty patterned petals on this cookie but you can also use this technique with sugarpaste.

1 Choose a selection of modelling paste colours. Knead well and roll long thin sausages of each colour. Depending on the scale of the patterns you want, either use a smoother to help you roll even sausages or a sugar shaper fitted with a round disc – see the Tools chapter for instructions on using this tool.

2 Choose one coloured sausage for the centre of the flower and place others in contrasting colours around this central core. I have used two colours to help make the petal effect more prominent. To help the pastes stick, smear a little clear alcohol or cooled boiled water over them to make them tacky.

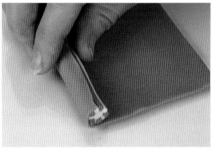

3 Thinly roll out modelling paste in either the same colour as one of the petals or in another colour. Place the combined sausages onto the paste and roll up, so the sausage is completely covered, and trim away the excess.

4 With a sharp craft knife, divide the sausage up into equal segments and stack these to produce a fatter, shorter sausage.

5 Roll the resulting paste to compress and adhere the paste. Then carefully, using a sharp knife, slice through the paste every 3mm (⅛in).

6 Place the slices next to one another and using a rolling pin, roll over the slices to thin the paste to 1.5mm (⅟₁₆in), using narrow spacers. If using this technique with sugarpaste you may find it easier to mount the sliced pattern onto a backing of sugarpaste before rolling over it to thin it, this gives the paste a little more strength and so makes it easier to handle.

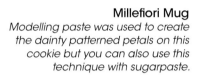

Tip
To make animal print, choose suitable colours and arrange the sausages around the core in an appropriate way for the animal print you wish to make.

Painting

I have always enjoyed painting on cakes – the paint colours seem to add an extra dimension, whether it be to the vibrancy of the design, subtlety of the pattern or the intricacy of the details. Sugarpaste forms the perfect canvas to experiment with painting skills but do not worry, as you will see in this chapter, you don't have to be a talented artist to create some very striking paint effects.

Chapter Contents:

Materials and equipment

To paint on cakes you will need a selection of good-quality paintbrushes in different sizes and widths plus a selection of edible colours. Edible colours are available in paste, powder and liquid forms. The liquid colours are often a little too wet for painting so I would recommend using paste and powder colours. Both paste and powder colours require the addition of a little cooled boiled water or clear alcohol (e.g. gin or vodka) to achieve the viscosity that is suitable for painting. If you wish to make your paint colours more opaque or whiter, add some edible whitening powder e.g. superwhite (SF). I often do this, especially when painting pictures.

Perfect Poppies

Once you know how to paint on sugarpaste anything is possible, as the delicate poppies on this vivid cake show. See the Projects chapter for step-by-step instructions for this cake, plus the materials lists and instructions for all the other cakes and cookies shown in this chapter.

Flood Painting

I have been using this technique to decorate the boards of my cakes for many years. It is really effective and unusual, yet is incredibly simple. You just need to allow yourself a few days for the resulting pattern to dry.

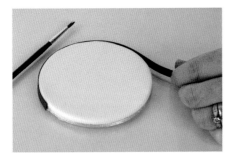

1 Cover a cake board with white sugarpaste. To help retain the liquid, add a thin border to the top or sides of the board using strips of thinly rolled modelling paste. Use a smoother to ensure the strips are straight and flush with the edge of the board. These are not strictly necessary for a round board, as the surface tension of the liquid holds it in place, but are essential for a square board.

2 Separately dilute your chosen edible paste colours slightly with cooled boiled water or clear alcohol. Take a paintbrush and roughly paint each colour in circular bands over the board leaving some areas white.

Tip
Try this effect on a spare piece of sugarpaste first – I assure you it is not as drastic as it sounds!

Cool Blues
The flood painting technique looks so effective on cake boards, especially if done in dark colours as a foil to a lighter cake.

3 Carefully pour clear alcohol or cooled boiled water over the partially painted surface then use a paintbrush to encourage the liquid to cover the board entirely. The liquid will melt the surface of the paste so that the colours merge – be patient, this takes a while.

4 Once the sugarpaste has turned syrupy – this will take between 30 minutes to an hour or perhaps longer depending on the temperature and humidity you are working in – take a cocktail stick (toothpick) or fine paintbrush and draw patterns through the sugar to transfer colour from one area to another. Leave undisturbed on a level surface to dry thoroughly.

Background Painting

Rather than leaving your sugarpaste surface plain why not intensify the colour or add textural interest, using one of the following techniques?

Stippling

Stippling is the applying of small dots of paint that together produce an even or softly graded shadow effect. You need a brush with reasonably firm bristles – too soft and the effect will not work, too hard and you could mark the paste. The size will depend on the area you wish to paint. In the example here, a fairly firm no. 10 artist's brush is used, however for cake boards or cakes use a round-headed brush about 2.5cm (1in) wide, as this will cover the surface more effectively.

Snowflake Stocking
Stippling is one of the easiest ways of adding colour.

1 Separately dilute your chosen edible paste colours with cooled boiled water or clear alcohol. I am using two tones of blue here. If your paste has been embossed as mine has, paint over the embossed area, allowing the colour to fill the indented shape. If painting a large area, complete a small section at a time, as you don't want the paint to dry at this stage.

2 Take a dry stippling brush and apply short vertical strokes over and around the embossed area to spread the colour and give a dotted appearance. Continue painting sections varying the shade and depth of colour.

Flat Surface If you are painting a flat sugarpaste surface, dip the stippling brush directly into the diluted edible paste colour, remove any excess moisture from the brush and use to stipple the sugarpaste.

Tip
Also try ragging using a twisted or bunched-up paper towel to create a textural pattern.

This Little Piggy…
The subtle blending on this cookie was created with a sponge.

Sponging

This is similar to stippling but uses a sponge to apply and remove paint. Natural sea sponges give more textured and interesting effects but try experimenting with synthetic sponges too.

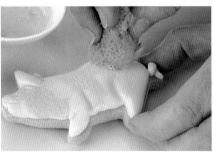

1 Separately dilute your chosen edible paste colours with cooled boiled water or clear alcohol. Here I am using a mixed peachy pink with a little whitener added to give a more opaque colour. Choose a sponge of a suitable size, dip it into your paint and apply to your sugarpaste surface using short vertical strokes.

2 Take a clean damp sponge and remove sections of paint to give a more blended appearance. Also try smudging the paint by stroking the paste with the sponge.

Colour Washes

An excellent way of adding subtle variations of colour to your cakes and cookies, colour washing is generally applied with brushes over a solid colour, using long sweeping strokes to blend and merge the colours together.

An Apple a Day
Tones of green were were added in sweeping strokes to the green sugarpaste base on this cookie, and the rouge was applied with very light sweeping strokes and a dry brush.

1 Cover your cookie, cake board or cake with sugarpaste of a suitable colour. Mix up your chosen colours of edible paint, and remember that you can make the colours more opaque using whitener. Apply the first colour in long sweeping strokes over a section of sugarpaste.

2 Continue adding other colours blending and merging the colours as you go. Do not try to add a further layer of colour on top of the first layer until it has dried. If you do you'll probably find that your brush removes most of the colour rather than adding to it – the exception to this is if you have added whitener to your edible paste colours.

Washes over an embossed surface

This technique is so simple yet so effective. I have used lace to texture my paste but many embossers work really well using this technique (see the Embossing chapter).

Killer Heels
The more detailed the embossed pattern, the more effective the finished result.

1 Emboss the surface of your sugarpaste and use to cover your cupcakes or cookies. If using this technique on a cake or board, texture the sugarpaste once in position. Dilute your chosen edible paste colour with clear alcohol and, using an appropriate sized brush, paint over all the textured sugarpaste, ensuring that the colour reaches all the indented areas. Leave to dry thoroughly.

2 Once dry, take a paper towel, dampen with clear alcohol and gently wipe away the paint colour from the uppermost surface of the sugarpaste to create a two-tone effect.

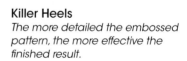

Tip
Don't make the sugarpaste too wet, otherwise the surface will melt and you could distort or lose your pattern. If this does start to happen, stop immediately and allow the paste to dry, then start afresh.

Painting a Picture Using Embossers

This technique is like painting by numbers – all the hard work is done for you and all you need to do is fill in the blanks! There are many embossers available, so chose ones that are a suitable size and have a design that appeals to you.

Out of This World
The alien and planet motifs fit the top of these cupcakes perfectly, but just using part of a design can also be very effective.

1 Emboss your sugarpaste with your chosen design. Separately dilute your chosen edible paste colours with cooled boiled water or clear alcohol and start to paint the sections of the same colour, varying the intensity if you wish.

2 Add other colours and further details as desired. For best results, you would be wise to practise first as you may need to let areas dry before adding abutting colours.

Edible Ink Pens

Edible ink pens are now widely available in a rainbow of colours, some are even double ended giving you two different tip sizes. The thicker tips are excellent for writing quick messages onto cakes or cookies or filling in shapes with colour, while the fine tips are great for adding fine details or accents to designs. The pens are used in the same way as a standard felt-tip pen and work best when used on light-coloured icing.

Drawing on sugarpaste

Cover your cake with sugarpaste and allow to dry. The firmer the sugarpaste surface the easier it is to use the pens. Take the cap off your chosen colour and write a message or draw and colour a design. In this example (taken from the cake at the start of this chapter), I have drawn a poppy onto a sponge-painted shape.

Tip

To ensure a good ink flow from your pens, store them upside down so that the ink runs into the nib. However, store double-ended pens horizontally.

Printing

Printing is the process of producing an image or shape by means of a tool, such as a stamp. The steps below show two methods, both on soft sugarpaste. For stamps, I have used the end of wooden dowels and sugarcraft embossers.

Using edible paste colours

Mix your edible paste colours to a fairly thick consistency with cooled boiled water or clear alcohol. Dip the stamp into a colour then, holding the stamp at right angles to your sugarpaste surface, gently lower and press to print the colour on. You may need to practise so that you exert the right amount of pressure and have the correct quantity of paint on your stamp. Repeat with other colours to create interesting patterns.

Desert Sunrise
These Aboriginal-art inspired cupcakes were created using simple circles stamped on with edible paste colours.

Using edible dust colours

This technique creates beautiful line images on your sugarpaste using embossers. Try experimenting using different types of embossers, as it is possible to add really fine details.

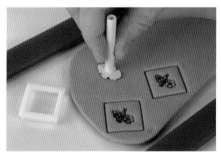

1 Select a suitable sugarcraft embosser and dip it into dry edible dust. Tap off the excess dust so that the embosser is evenly coated. If edible dust is trapped in a small section of the embosser, use a suitable sized paintbrush to remove it – if you don't you will have a blob of colour on your finished piece rather than a delicate outline.

2 Holding the stamp at right angles to your sugarpaste surface, gently press the embosser into the sugarpaste. The dust will transfer from the edges of the embosser to the soft sugarpaste creating a beautifully coloured outline design.

3 It may be necessary, especially if you are using a larger embosser, to press gently around the embossed design with a finger or smoother to close the indented gap, this will make the design crisper.

Tip
Experiment with different colours of dusts and sugarpaste to see which you find most effective.

Patchwork Prints
Detailed mini-embossers were used with edible dust colours to print the fine designs on these cupcakes.

Transferring an Image

Not many people feel confident enough to paint freehand directly onto a cake. So, the easiest way around this is to transfer the outline of the image you wish to paint onto your sugarpaste surface. There are a number of options available to you, but firstly, you will need to decide what you would like to paint and then you may need to resize your design or images to suit your cake. Of the three methods that follow, the first two are effective on dried sugarpaste, and the third is best on fresh sugarpaste.

Using a scriber

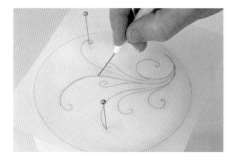

1 Trace your design onto wax or parchment paper and pin or hold the design onto the cake. Trace the scriber over all the lines on the design, with enough pressure to mark the sugarpaste surface of the cake below.

2 Carefully remove the paper, the design should now appear as a faint outline. This method works well for outlining shapes but is not so easy to use on complex designs or small details.

Using a pin or pouncing wheel

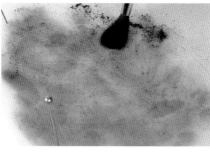

1 Place wax or parchment paper over your design and place onto a cutting board or corrugated cardboard. Secure in place then using a pin or pouncing wheel prick little holes through the paper along the lines of the design. The more detailed the design, the closer together and more holes you will need.

2 Place the parchment paper over the cake and depending on the colour of the icing, use a small soft brush to force edible dust colour through the holes.

3 Remove the paper and your design is now on the cake. This technique can be used for quite complex and detailed designs.

Using edible pens

1 Carefully trace the reverse of your desired design or images onto wax or parchment paper with edible ink pens. Soon after you have traced a line the ink will separate and form a series of dots, this is perfectly normal!

2 Immediately flip the design over onto the top or sides of your cake. Using a smoother, carefully rub the back of the paper onto the cake surface so that the design transfers onto the cake.

3 Gently pull the paper away to reveal the transferred design. This method works best on a freshly covered cake, as the icing takes up the colour transfer better, however this technique is possible on a dried sugarpaste surface too.

Painting an Image

For best results, paint your picture in stages so that the paint has a chance to dry – this prevents colours running into each other and allows you to add different colours on top of each other.

Tip
Before painting the real thing, it's always wise to practise on a spare piece of sugarpaste to experiment with colours and techniques.

1 Mix your choice of edible paste colours with clear alcohol and select a range of suitable brushes. Apply washes or colour blocks to sections of your design, starting from the background working forwards, allowing one section to dry before adding abutting sections. On my example, I painted the windows before the red body of the bus and the roofs and windows of the buildings before the walls.

2 Using a good-quality fine paintbrush, add fine details on top of all the painted sections – this is what really makes a picture come to life.

London Calling
To paint this design, I created a montage of pictures on the computer and resized them to fit snugly around the cake, then used the edible ink pen method to transfer the image.

Metallic Finishes

Add sparkle and opulence to your cakes and cookies using one of the following methods:

Edible lustre dusts

Edible lustre or metallic dusts are available in an array of colours that can be easily mixed and blended. There are a number of ways of applying these to the surface of your sugarpaste depending on the effect you require. For best results, before you begin, always colour your sugarpaste to a similar colour to the dust – this will help to intensify the colour and will prevent the finish looking streaky.

Midas Touch
Metallic dust gives instant decadence to these swirl-design cupcakes.

Method 1 Dust over a freshly covered cake with a large, soft dusting brush and edible metallic dust. This will give a beautiful lustre finish to your sugarpaste. It does not work well on sugarpaste that has crusted over, see Method 2.

Method 2 Smear white vegetable fat (shortening) over crusted sugarpaste and apply the dust over the fat with a large, soft dusting brush. This will give an intense colour, which can (depending on the brand of dust) be burnished to really glisten.

Method 3 Mix the edible lustre dust with clear alcohol to create a thick paint and use this to paint your cakes. Alternatively you can mix the dust with confectioners' glaze for even greater shine.

Gold leaf

24-carat gold leaf transfer makes a stunning statement on cakes and cookies as it reflects light beautifully. It is a very delicate material to use so give yourself plenty of time.

Bottle of Bubbly
Gold leaf provides the shimmering finishing touch on this fun cookie.

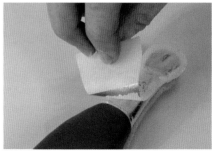

1 Draw your chosen shape on the back of the gold leaf transfer sheet. Carefully cut out the shape using sharp scissors, avoiding excessive finger contact with the gold.

2 Thinly brush the surface of your icing with sugar glue or confectioners' glaze, slightly larger than your shape. Allow the glue or glaze to go tacky. Do not rush – if the glue is still wet the gold will not transfer cleanly. Position the transfer accurately and press gently – it cannot be repositioned, so be careful.

3 Leave in place for a minute or two then peel off the backing paper with your fingers or tweezers using a slow upward movement. Allow to dry.

Stencilling

Stencilling is an extremely effective way to add impressive decorations to your cakes and cookies quickly. For the best and most satisfying results, I recommend you use laser-cut culinary stencils made from durable food-grade plastic. How you choose to add a stencilled pattern will depend on the effect you wish to achieve and the size of the item to be stencilled. This chapter shows you various techniques using both edible dusts and royal icing; it also shows you how to make your own stencils and some possible other uses.

Chapter Contents:

Culinary Stencils

Using Edible Dusts

★ Metallic lustre dusts

★ Matt dusts

★ Multicolour matt dusts

Using Royal Icing

★ On cookies

★ On cupcakes

★ On the tops of boards and cakes

★ On the sides of cakes

★ Multicolour effects

Adjusting a Stencil to Fit

Adding Embellishments

Making Your Own Stencil

★ Using readily available materials

★ Using specialist tools

Other Uses for Stencils

Stacked Hatboxes
The beautiful, intricate patterns on these boxes are created simply using culinary stencils, royal icing and edible dusts. See the Projects chapter for step-by-step instructions for this cake, plus the materials lists and instructions for all the other cakes and cookies shown in this chapter.

Culinary Stencils

There is a huge selection of culinary stencils available, so choosing a design can sometimes be a little tricky. The first consideration is the scale of the item you wish to decorate. You will need a much smaller-scale pattern for stencilling a cookie or cupcake than for a cake board. However, using part of a larger pattern on a cupcake or cookie can work very effectively, and repeating a small-scale pattern around the edge of a cake board is often very successful.

Using Edible Dusts

When using dusts to stencil your cakes and cookies, it is very important to ensure that the products you are using are edible. Read the small print on the pots of dusts that you have to make sure that the ones you are using are not for decoration purposes only. If they are edible they will have an ingredients list and a best before date.

Silver Swirls
These glamorous cookies were created using edible metallic dust, which gives a very contemporary feel.

Metallic lustre dusts

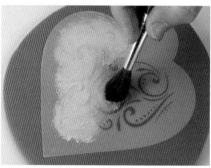

1 Roll out the sugarpaste to a thickness of 5mm (³⁄₁₆in), ideally using spacers. Place your chosen stencil on top of the sugarpaste. To ensure clean, sharp edges, place a smoother on top of the stencil and press down firmly so that the sugarpaste is forced up to the upper surface of the stencil.

2 Next, smear a thin layer of white vegetable fat (shortening) over the surface of the sugarpaste pattern i.e. the paste that has been forced up through the stencil. Use either a finger or a suitable paintbrush to do this.

3 Take a large, soft dusting brush and dip it into the edible lustre dust, knock off any excess then liberally dust over the stencil, adding more dust as needed. Brush off any excess dust from the stencil – this ensures that as you lift the stencil no stray dust falls from it, spoiling the pattern beneath. Use the brush to burnish the dust (if the product allows) to make it really shine.

4 Carefully lift the stencil away from the paste to reveal the pattern. You may need to use two hands to do this.

5 Cut out a shape using the same cutter that you used to make the cookie. Remove the excess paste from around the shape. Then, using a cranked handled palette knife and a quick swipe action so as not to distort the shape, position the knife under the sugarpaste.

6 Carefully lift the stencilled sugarpaste shape and position it onto a cookie that has been covered with piping gel. Remove the palette knife and, if necessary, using a clean finger, press the paste so it is all in contact with the cookie. If you need to do this more than once, ensure that your fingers are clean, as you do not want to spoil the pattern.

Tip

Use a soft brush to achieve a uniform finish – if the bristles are too firm they may leave marks on the surface.

Matt dusts

1 Roll out the sugarpaste to a thickness of 5mm (³⁄₁₆in), ideally using spacers. Place your stencil on top of the sugarpaste. Using a smoother, gently press onto the stencil just enough to prevent it moving.

2 Mix edible dust colours to create a suitable shade – I have used a dark pink and white to create a mid-pink. Dip your brush into the dust, knock off any excess then carefully dust over the stencil. Vary the intensity of colour by adding more or less dust to various sections of the pattern as desired. Brush off any excess dust from the stencil – this ensures that as you lift the stencil no stray dust falls from it, spoiling the pattern beneath.

3 Carefully lift the stencil to reveal the pattern. Cut out a circle from the stencilled sugarpaste to fit the top of your cupcake then gently lift it and position onto a cupcake using a palette knife. If necessary, press the paste with a clean finger so it is all in contact with the cupcake. Make sure you use a clean finger each time you do this, so that you don't spoil the pattern.

Love Hearts
Matt dusts were used to create this soft, romantic design.

Multicolour matt dusts

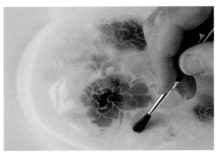

1 Roll out the sugarpaste as for matt dusts. Mix different dusts to create suitable colours. Dip a soft brush into one of the dusts, knock off any excess then carefully dust over sections of the stencil, varying the intensity of colour by adding more or less dust. For example, dust the centre of the flower with dark purple then add a light dusting to some of the petals and the edges of leaves.

2 Take a clean brush, dip it into another colour and carefully dust over new sections of the pattern. For example, add some light pink to the outer petals of the flower. Add as many colours to your stencil as you wish, but try to use clean brushes when changing colour and remove all excess dust between colours to ensure that they do not become muddy.

3 Carefully lift the stencil away from the paste to reveal the pattern. Add to the cupcake, as described in step 3 of matt dusts above.

Perfect Peonies
A range of different coloured matt dusts were used to create this stunning cupcake.

Using Royal Icing

The secret to using royal icing (see the Sugar Recipes, section) on stencils is to make your icing the correct consistency. You should aim to have a reasonably stiff soft peak icing that will not seep under the stencil or flood the stencilled pattern once the stencil is removed. To adjust the consistency, either add icing (confectioners') sugar to thicken it or cooled boiled water to soften it. Experiment on a spare piece of sugarpaste before you stencil directly onto a cake or board. You will find that some stencil patterns are more forgiving than others but generally the finer and closer the detail, the stiffer the icing must be to achieve a really good result.

Wonky Wedding
The 'tiers' of this wonky cake cookie can be decorated with an endless variety of colours and designs, so don't be afraid to experiment and create something unique.

On cookies

1 Roll out the sugarpaste to a thickness of 5mm (³⁄₁₆in). Cut out the shape using the cookie cutter, but leave the surrounding paste in place so that the stencil lies flat. Place the stencil on top and use a palette knife to spread royal icing carefully over the relevant section. Use one or two strokes going from side to side. Do not lift the knife as this may cause the stencil to lift and smudge the pattern.

2 Once the icing is of an even thickness, carefully remove the stencil. The thickness of the royal icing is very much personal preference. If it is applied thinly then interesting two-tone effects can be created where the sugarpaste colour is visible through the icing. If the icing is applied more thickly then the pattern has a more three-dimensional textured effect.

3 Using a palette knife, if required, cut the stencilled paste to the required shape. For this example, cut the lower tier of the wonky cake from the upper tiers. Remove all the excess sugarpaste from around the stencilled shape. Paint piping gel over the cookie to act as glue.

4 Using a clean palette knife and a quick swipe action so as not to distort the shape, position the knife under the sugarpaste before carefully lifting the shape and placing it on top of the cookie. Repeat using other colours of sugarpaste and royal icing, choosing colour combinations and stencil patterns that complement each other.

Tip
To clean your stencils, place them in a bowl of water to dissolve the royal icing and then pat them dry.

On cupcakes

1 Roll out the sugarpaste to a thickness of 5mm (³⁄₁₆in). Cut out a circle to fit the top of your cupcake, but leave the surrounding paste in place so that the stencil lies flat. Place the stencil on top and use a palette knife to spread royal icing over the relevant section. Use one or two strokes going from side to side. Do not lift the knife as this may cause the stencil to lift and smudge the pattern.

2 Once the royal icing is of an even thickness, remove the stencil and peel away the excess sugarpaste.

Tip

If using white royal icing, add a little superwhite dust to give an opaque rather than a translucent finish.

Tea at the Ritz
Using white royal icing on a coloured background creates a stylish cupcake, set off by metallic high tea cupcake cases.

3 Using a cranked handled palette knife and a quick swipe action, position the knife under the sugarpaste circle and carefully lift and place it on top of the cupcake. Leave for a few minutes to allow the royal icing to dry – try to avoid the temptation to touch it.

4 The sugarpaste circle should more or less have fallen into place, however it may be necessary to press down the edges of the circle gently so they are in full contact with the cupcake. Doing this once the royal icing has dried prevents the pattern being distorted or smudged.

On the tops of boards and cakes

Whether you wish to cover the top of a cake or a cake board the same principles apply. Choose a suitable stencil and follow the steps here. For cake boards you can use a stencil that is larger than the board. You will have to tidy up the edges of the pattern but this can be done quickly and effectively with a damp brush.

1 Colour some royal icing to complement your colour scheme using edible paste or liquid colours. Place your chosen stencil centrally on the covered cake or board, then place your icing in the centre of the stencil so the weight of the icing acts as an anchor, preventing the stencil from moving.

2 Using either a cranked handled palette knife or the longer straight edge of a side scraper, carefully begin spreading the icing out from the centre using radial strokes that go right to the edge of the stencil. Remove any excess icing that remains on your knife or scraper at the end of each stroke.

3 Once the stencil is completely covered, work towards achieving an even thickness of icing, removing any excess with more careful strokes. Once you are happy with the finish, peel away the stencil carefully.

Tip
A slight error in a royal iced stencilled pattern can be corrected with a damp paintbrush while the icing is still wet.

Pretty in Pink
This peony cake is decorated subtly using royal icing just a few shades darker than the sugarpaste, but you could choose to use a contrasting colour for a more dramatic statement.

On the sides of cakes

Adding a stencil to the side of a cake can be challenging. There are two methods: firstly by adding the stencilled pattern directly to the side of a cake using royal icing, and secondly by stencilling a strip of modelling paste with edible dusts or royal icing and then attaching this to the side of a cake. The method you choose will depend on the result you wish to achieve and the stencil pattern itself. Wrap the stencil around the side of your cake and if you find that sections of the design are sticking out from the side of the cake then the best policy is to stencil a modelling paste strip. Once stencilled, the strip can be transferred to the side of your cake with the help of an extra pair of hands – this was the method used in the middle tier of the Stacked Hatboxes cake shown at the start of the chapter. The following steps show stencilling being added directly to the side of a cake.

Tip
Practise this technique on a cake dummy or cake tin before you try it on an actual cake.

1 Ensure that the sides of your cake are vertical using a set square when covering your cake (see the Covering Cakes and Boards section) then allow the icing to set. Use a stencil side fixing kit to secure the stencil in place. You might also find it helpful to insert a couple of pins at one end of the stencil to prevent movement.

2 Take a side scraper and load it with royal icing then, starting at the end of the stencil secured with pins, carefully begin spreading the icing along the stencil. Add more icing as necessary, ensuring that the pattern is completely covered. Try to achieve an even thickness of icing, removing any excess with careful strokes.

3 Once you are happy with the finish, carefully remove the pins and undo the fixing kit to reveal the pattern. If you wish to add another section of stencil design, allow the royal icing to dry before repeating the process.

Side to Side
To decorate the different tiers in the Stacked Hatboxes cake, you will need to use your chosen stencils a number of times, adjusting them to fit using the techniques described in this chapter.

Multicolour effects

Exciting multicolour effects can be created using different colours of royal icing on one stencil. The colours are simply blended together so that each time the process is repeated the results are slightly different – perfect for a set of cupcakes or cookies, as each one will be similar but unique.

Geisha Girls
This Japanese-inspired design was stencilled using different shades of pink icing from very pale to very bold.

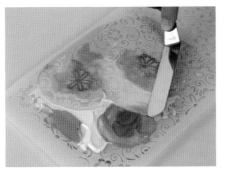

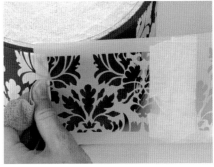

1 Separately colour small amounts of royal icing, using superwhite dust to whiten, if necessary, and edible paste or liquid colours to colour. Lay your stencil over your rolled-out sugarpaste then add dollops of different colours to different sections of the stencil, ideally using different palette knives for speed.

2 Take a clean palette knife and, using a few careful strokes, spread and merge the colours of the royal icing. The way in which you do this will determine how the colours are distributed over the stencil, so carefully consider the effect that you are aiming for before you start spreading the icing.

3 Once you are happy with the effect and the icing is of an even thickness, carefully remove the stencil. If you wish to decorate a whole batch of cupcakes, for example, allow enough royal icing of each colour – you can reuse the excess icing you remove from each stencil but your colours may not be as distinct.

Adjusting a Stencil to Fit

You will often find that your chosen stencil design is not quite the right size or shape for your cake. If so, adjust it to fit using pattern repeat or masking techniques, which can be used separately or together as necessary.

Tip
Clean, dry and store your stencils carefully to ensure that they stay in tip-top condition.

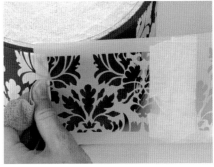

Pattern Repeat This is particularly useful when stencilling the side of a cake and most side stencils are designed in such a way that any join in the pattern looks seamless. The secret is to allow the first pattern to dry and to wash and dry the stencil before attempting the repeat. When ready, position the stencil so that the pattern looks continuous and apply royal icing as previously described.

Masking This may be necessary when using pattern repeats around a cake to ensure that you have a perfect fit. It is also necessary when you wish to use only part of a stencil design. To mask a stencil, simply cover the areas of the design around the section you wish to use with masking tape. This allows you to spread the icing without accidentally stencilling more of the pattern than you intended.

Adding Embellishments

Beautiful stencilled patterns can easily be enhanced to create sugar pieces that are truly stunning. Here are a couple of simple ideas to get you started.

Designer Daisies
These cookies can be embellished to your heart's content. Here, cut outs have been used together with a scroll stencil.

Piping Try adding a few piped royal icing dots in either the same, a tonal or a contrasting colour (see the Piping chapter). These can be piped around or on top of the stencilled pattern to great effect. Try experimenting on a spare piece of sugarpaste to see how you can easily change the look and impact of a stencilled pattern with piped dots.

Cut Outs Adding more colour and texture to a stencilled pattern using cut outs is highly effective. Choose your colours carefully and think about scale – you want to create the illusion that the pattern and cut out are one. Don't be afraid to experiment – a cut out can easily be removed if it isn't working (see the Cutters chapter).

Moulds Using a moulded embellishment (see the Moulds chapter) is a fast and effective way to add more colour and interest to your stencilled pattern. Try experimenting with moulded shapes or flowers to see what works with your design.

Making Your Own Stencil

If you can't find a suitable stencil or you really want to personalize a cake, then making your own stencil may be the answer. You can either use readily available materials or use specialized stencil tools.

Tiers of Joy
Don't be limited by the range of commercial stencils when you can make your own.

Using readily available materials

You will need material from which to cut the stencil and some form of cutter. The example here uses card, a craft knife and a paper punch but try experimenting with other materials that you may have to hand.

Craft Knife Draw or transfer your design – here I have drawn with a pencil onto card, however you could easily trace an appropriate image or logo. Place the card onto a cutting mat or suitable surface and use a craft knife to cut away sections of the design.

Paper Punches General craft punches work really well if you want a design near the edge of your stencil, but note that not all punches will cut through card, so you may need to use another material such as waxed paper, which is not as durable.

Using specialist tools

You will need a plastic stencil sheet and a stencil tool, which you use to melt the sheet to create your stencil.

1 Place your design under your plastic stencil sheet and secure with tape. Heat up the stencil tool – this usually takes about five minutes. The tip of the tool gets extremely hot so be very careful to prevent any accidental burning. Always read and follow the manufacturer's instructions carefully.

2 Hold the tool in your hand so the nib is vertical and your hand is resting on your work surface, as if you were writing. Trace around your design quickly and smoothly, applying just enough pressure to feel the surface below the tip (the cut is made with heat, not pressure). Try not to linger at any point, as continuous heat could damage the stencil.

3 As with any technique, you'll find that you improve with practice so try out the tool on small designs first before embarking on a larger project. Once you are happy with your design, use your stencil as described elsewhere in this chapter.

Logolicious!
The Lindy's Cakes logo motif on this cupcake was cut from a plastic stencil sheet with a heat tool.

Other Uses for Stencils

Another way of using stencils is to use them to emboss sugarpaste. I find this particularly useful if I want to add a subtle pattern to a large area such as a cake board, where the paste is embossed in situ, but it also works well on smaller-scale items such as cookies and cupcakes.

Funky Flip Flops
These cookies have been embossed using a stencil to leave a distinctive raised pattern on the soles.

1 Roll out the sugarpaste to a thickness of 5mm (³⁄₁₆in), ideally using spacers. Place your stencil on top of the paste. Using a smoother, press down firmly so that the sugarpaste is forced up to the upper surface of the stencil. Repeat for the remainder of the pattern.

2 Carefully remove the stencil and, if required, reposition and repeat, before cutting out shapes with your chosen cutters.

Cutters

Using cutters to create shapes is an easy and effective way to decorate your cakes and cookies. Be creative: repeat shapes, layer them up, abut sections to create new shapes or inlay one shape inside another. Try thinking outside the box – you may be using a petal cutter but does it have to represent a petal? What patterns can you create using just one shape? What happens when you combine an asymmetric shape with its mirror image? Look not only at the patterns of shapes you create but also at the spaces in between those shapes.

Chapter Contents:

All About Cutters

★ Plastic cutters

★ Metal cutters

Creating Cut-Out Shapes

★ Cutting simple shapes

★ Cutting intricate shapes

Layering

★ Using a single cutter

★ Using several cutters

Abutting

Inlay Work

Mosaic

Tip

Inspiration is all around you – look at designs on cards, gift wrap, curtain fabric, clothing, buildings, wrought-iron railings, stained-glass windows … Be inspired and don't just copy!

Flower Power

A host of different cutters were used to create the flowers and the banding on this loud and proud cake design. Go wild and see what you can create! See the Projects chapter for step-by-step instructions for this cake, plus the materials lists and instructions for all the other cakes shown in this chapter.

All About Cutters

There are a whole host of specialist sugarcraft cutters available – which you choose will depend on your preferences and the shapes you are trying to create.

Plastic cutters

These are usually manufactured in large quantities so tend to be available in the basic shapes and sizes that most cake decorators require, e.g. hearts and flower shapes. They have the advantage that they do not become misshapen with use, however they have to be stored carefully as their cutting edges can become damaged by other tools and cutters. The quality of cutting edges also varies and they are often not as sharp as fine metal equivalents.

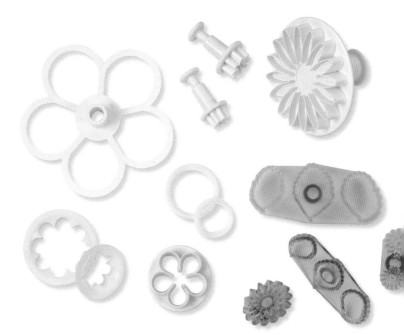

Metal cutters

There is a vast array of metal cutter designs available. Quality varies so buy the best you can afford. Cheaper cutters are often made from tin plate, which means that they have to be kept dry to prevent them rusting. Don't be tempted to leave them to air dry once washed; either dry thoroughly with a cloth or pop them in a warm oven to remove moisture. Stainless steel cutters on the other hand are easier to care for as they can be washed in a dishwasher, however they do have a higher price tag. Metal cutters also come in a variety of metal gauges; thinner gauges give a sharper cutting edge but become misshapen more readily while thicker gauges are more robust but tend not to cut as well.

Creating Cut-Out Shapes

Cut outs are very simple to create, just use thinly rolled modelling paste and your choice of cutters. I usually recommend that your paste be 1.5mm (¹⁄₁₆in) thick and that you use spacers to help you achieve an even thickness, however sometimes a design calls for thinner paste and at other times a chunkier look is more appropriate. The steps here show you how to use a selection of different cutters.

Love Is...
... simple cut-out shapes on a delicious cupcake!

Cutting simple shapes

1 Roll out your modelling paste between narrow spacers, ideally on a non-stick work board. Press your chosen cutter into the paste. It may help to give the cutter a gentle wiggle as this ensures it cuts all the way through the paste – this is especially important when using plastic cutters.

2 Remove the excess paste and leave the cut shape to firm up for a moment or two – this helps prevent the shape distorting. Remove the shape from your board by sliding a palette knife underneath. If the edges of your shape are feathered, as can happen with some cutters, press these underneath with a finger before adding to your cake using sugar glue.

Plunger Cutters These are usually very successful at cutting out clean shapes. Press your chosen plunger into your rolled-out modelling paste, wiggle the cutter quickly from side to side. Lift the cutter (the paste should come up with it) rub your finger over the cutter to remove any small flecks of paste, then press down on the plunger to release the shape.

Piping Tubes (Tips) These can make excellent small cutters – I find the plain round ones particularly useful. Place your selected tube on your forefinger and use as a cutter by pressing into freshly rolled modelling paste. If the paste is picked up by the tube, use a soft paintbrush to push it out.

Cutting intricate shapes

1 To get a clean cut, rather than pressing the cutter into the modelling paste, place the paste over the cutter and roll over with a rolling pin.

2 Run your finger over the edges of the cutter, then turn the cutter over and carefully press out the paste using a soft paintbrush.

Layering

Many of my cake designs are built up in layers – they might look complicated at first glance but if you deconstruct the elements, they are created from simple shapes placed one on top of another.

Rajasthan Rose
Two different flower cut outs are layered on this mini-cake, with a third shape embossed into the paste.

Using a single cutter

1 To create layers of the same shape, one slightly larger than the other, without having two different cutters, roll out two different colours of modelling paste between narrow spacers and cut out shapes using the same cutter. Place a smoother over shapes of one colour and press down on the paste to enlarge them fractionally.

2 Paint sugar glue over the enlarged shapes then, using a palette knife or paintbrush, lift the shapes of the second colour and place carefully over the first so that a rim of the larger shape is visible around the edge. Attach in place on your cake.

Using several cutters

Cut out modelling paste shapes in differing sizes and colours, following the instructions on the previous page. Arrange the shapes one layer at a time on top of each other, using sugar glue or water to secure. The photo above uses four layers, the mini-cake, top, uses shapes in three layers while the Flower Power cake at the start of the chapter uses five layers. Experiment to see which shapes, sizes and colours work for you.

Tip

Knead your modelling paste to warm it up before rolling it out. If the paste is a bit hard or too crumbly, add a little white vegetable fat (shortening) and/ or cooled boiled water to soften it – it should be firm but with some elasticity.

Abutting

Abutting simple shapes can be a really successful way of creating amazing patterns. In its simplest form, this technique is placing one shape next to another so edges of both shapes are adjacent. However, shapes do not always fit snugly together so to abut the paste one shape is cut into, using the cutter from the adjoining shape. This may take a little time and patience – especially if you are attempting intricate designs – but persevere, as the results can be stunning. The steps here show you how to create rows of abutting shapes using one circle cutter, however you can use this technique using as many or as few cutters as you like and abut just two shapes or cover a whole cake.

Tip

To use this technique on cupcakes, create the pattern on freshly rolled sugarpaste and cut out circles to fit your cupcakes.

1 Roll out some modelling paste between narrow spacers to ensure a uniform thickness. Cut out a number of circles, then cut each in half and arrange around the lower edge of a cake so that the straight edges lie against the board and the circles just touch each other.

2 Next, roll out another colour of modelling paste to the same thickness as the first and cut a row of circles so that they just touch. Using the same cutter, cut the next row as shown. Add the resulting shapes to your cake to create the second row.

3 Repeat this process in another modelling paste colour, recreating the rows of circles before cutting the required shapes to ensure that the shapes will fit snugly against the previous row. Repeat, creating as many rows as required.

Orient Express
You don't need lots of fancy cutters to create stunning patterns – this design was made with just one circle cutter, topped with layered flowers made from simple blossom cutters.

Inlay Work

This technique involves using cutters to insert one shape inside another to create a design. Small designs, such as the one shown here, can be created on your work board before being transferred to a cake. For larger designs it is often more prudent to create these directly on your cake, making sure that the icing surface is as firm as possible and that you apply sugar glue only to sections that are not being removed and replaced.

Tip
Remember that piping tubes (tips) make excellent small circle cutters.

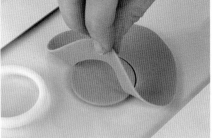

1 Individually roll out the different colours of modelling paste between narrow spacers and cover with plastic or a stay-fresh mat to prevent them drying out. Using the largest circle cutter cut a circle from one of the rolled-out pastes. Leave the circle where it was cut – this prevents the circle distorting – and carefully remove the excess paste.

2 Take a slightly smaller circle cutter and centrally remove a circle from the larger circle. A scriber is an excellent tool to help remove the cut circles not required.

3 Replace this circle with one of a different colour and blend the join between the two circles by rubbing a finger over the pastes so that there is no gap between them. Continue like this, removing and replacing circles of different colours.

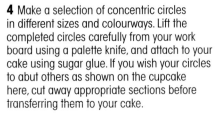

4 Make a selection of concentric circles in different sizes and colourways. Lift the completed circles carefully from your work board using a palette knife, and attach to your cake using sugar glue. If you wish your circles to abut others as shown on the cupcake here, cut away appropriate sections before transferring them to your cake.

Ever-Decreasing Circles
Circles of modelling paste are inlaid to create this striking geometric design.

Mosaic

Creating mosaics in sugar works extremely well, you'll just need a little drying time between each stage. Create your pattern using cutters of different sizes and shapes, cutting larger shapes into pieces to create more tiles. For inspiration, look at the stunning work of architect Antoni Gaudi – a true mosaic master. The steps here describe how to create a multicoloured flower on a blue and green background, but the techniques are similar whatever design you wish to create.

Mosaic Marvel
Use modelling paste to create your design, then 'grout' the tiles with softened sugarpaste.

1 Knead a selection of modelling paste colours. Roll out the pastes between narrow spacers so that the mosaic tiles are all of the same thickness. Cut out petals from your chosen colours and arrange on your covered cake or board.

2 To create the background tiles, roll out some more modelling paste of a different colour or colours. Then, using the cutters used to create the design, recreate a small section of the design in the background colour. Remove the cut shapes then, using a craft knife or cutting wheel, cut the remaining shapes to create tiles to fit the background spaces.

3 Lift and separate some of the cut mosaic tiles using a palette knife then, using a damp brush, place the tiles into a suitable position on your cake or board, making sure you leave a small gap between each tile. Trim to size once in position, if necessary. Allow the tiles to dry thoroughly.

4 When dry, take a contrasting sugarpaste colour – I have used white – and place a little onto your work board. Add some cooled boiled water and blend together with a palette knife. Add more sugarpaste and more water until the paste has a soft spreadable consistency.

5 Working in sections, spread the softened sugarpaste over the dried tiles so that the paste fills all the gaps between the tiles. Remove as much excess paste as possible with the palette knife.

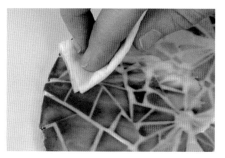

6 Using a folded damp paper towel, carefully remove the remaining paste from the surface of the tiles and allow to dry. Repeat until all sections are complete.

Flowers

Flowers are probably the most popular choice of all cake decorations. There are many books written on the art of sugar flower making, but I can only just touch on this subject here. The simplest representation of a flower is a cut-out shape (see the Cutters chapter). Other more interesting ways of representing flowers are to create fabric-effect flowers out of paste or try your hand at creating lifelike flowers.

Chapter Contents:

Fabric Flowers

★ Rose

★ Blossom

★ Dahlia

Simple Cupped Flower

Lifelike Flowers

★ Poppy

★ Peony

Tip
Whether you choose to add simple cut-out flowers or full-sized lifelike blooms will depend on the look you are after and the time you have available.

Fuchsia Fashionista
Three-dimensional fabric-effect roses, dahlias and blossoms are used to decorate this gorgeous handbag cake that will make any fashion-conscious woman drool! See the Projects chapter for step-by-step instructions for this cake, plus the materials lists and instructions for all the other cakes shown in this chapter.

Fabric Flowers

Many craft ideas are interchangeable, many are adaptable and this is certainly true of fabric flowers. Here are three examples that are often made from fabric or leather but are highly effective when made from sugar and added to cakes. All you will need to create them is some thinly rolled modelling paste. The paste can be textured with a fabric-effect rolling pin or similar for more authenticity if you wish.

Tender Roses
Fabric-effect roses in warm shades set the tone for this romantic cupcake.

Rose

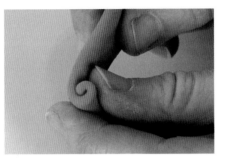

Rose

1 Thinly roll out your modelling paste. Make sure your paste is firm yet stretchy – add a little white vegetable fat (shortening) and/or cooled boiled water if it is a little dry or doesn't have enough stretch. Fold over a section of paste and cut the fold to a width of 1.5cm (½in) for a small rose, 7cm (2¾in) for a large rose or somewhere in between.

2 Starting at one end of the folded paste, roll up the paste to form a spiral.

Blossom

Dahlia

3 Press the cut edges together as you go and gather the paste slightly as you roll to create fullness and space in the flower.

4 Finally, neaten the back of the rose by cutting off the excess paste with scissors.

Fabric Flowers
The cake at the start of this chapter features all of these flowers on a realistic handbag design. Try arrangements of different combinations of flowers to see what different effects can be achieved.

Blossom

To create this flower you will also need an oval cutter – the size of the cutter determines the size of the resulting flower.

Pretty Pastels
Arrange blossoms in groups of three to create this sweet and simple cupcake design.

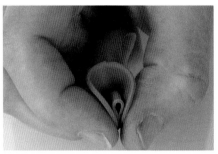

1 Thinly roll out the modelling paste between narrow spacers and cut out six ovals per flower. Pick up one of the oval shapes, holding it between the thumb and forefinger of one hand, then with your other hand, lift up the centre of one side of the oval.

2 Remove your finger from the centre and bring your thumb and forefinger together. Press the paste firmly so the created petal sticks to itself. Repeat for the remaining petals.

3 Using a paintbrush and some sugar glue, stick the petals together to form a circle. Finally, roll a ball of paste and attach it to the centre of the flower using sugar glue.

Dahlia

All you need to create this flower is some modelling paste, a quilting tool and a circle cutter. The size of the cutter determines the size of the resulting flower – try different sizes to see which you think are suitable.

Darling Dahlia
A fabric-effect dahlia made using a small circle cutter adorns this cupcake. Try using modelling paste to tone with the paper cases, or go for greater contrast, as here.

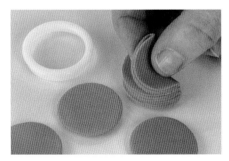

1 Thinly roll out modelling paste between narrow spacers and cut out eight circles per flower. Fold each circle in half and stack the folding circles together using a little sugar glue – don't add too much though as you want the folded paste to stick, not slide.

2 Place the stuck circles on their folds, ease open the stack and bring the two ends together, then glue in place. Adjust the flower so that the petals are evenly spaced.

3 Take a quilting tool and run the wheel down the centre of each petal to add a stitching line. Allow the paste to firm up slightly before adding the flower to your cake.

Simple Cupped Flower

These can be made very easily – you just need some modelling paste or flower paste, a petal cutter, a ball tool and foam pad, and a former.

Tip
If you don't have a foam pad you can just use the palm of your hand.

1 Thinly roll out the modelling paste and cut out a number of petals, how many will depend on the petal cutter you are using and how full you want your flower to appear. In my example I have used six petals.

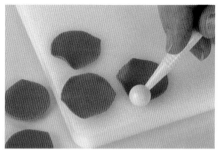

2 When you use cutters to cut out leaves and petals, there is always a sharp cut edge to remove. Place your petals onto a foam pad then take the ball tool and stroke around the edges of the paste by pressing the tool half on the paste and half on the pad to soften them. To frill the petal edges slightly, push a little more firmly so the paste thins and start to frill.

3 To enable the flower to dry in its cupped shape you will need a former. Ready-made polystyrene formers in a number of sizes are commercially available for this but you can easily make your own former using aluminium foil cupped over the top of a round pastry cutter, cup, glass or any other object with a circular rim.

4 Arrange the petals in the former so that they overlap. Use a touch of sugar glue to secure them in place. There are many ways of adding flower centres – in this example I have simply rolled lots of modelling paste balls, coloured to match the cake, and attached these with a little sugar glue.

Floral Elegance
A simple cupped flower on top of a mini-cake transforms it into a thing of beauty.

Lifelike Flowers

These flowers are made from flower paste, as this can be rolled out very thinly and dries hard. Flowers made from flower paste retain their shape and are not as badly affected by moisture as flowers made from other pastes. Be aware though that dried flower paste is very brittle so handle your flowers with the utmost care. These flowers, although technically edible, are not good to eat but do make wonderful keepsakes.

So Convincing
The sugar poppy on the Perfect Poppies cake in the Painting chapter is so realistic you would be forgiven for thinking it was a real flower!

Poppy

I love the brilliance yet simplicity of poppies, their petals may be almost any colour so can be added to cakes with many different colour schemes. Poppies usually have between four and six petals. To create this bright red poppy you will need red, green and black flower paste, a poppy petal cutter, a double-sided poppy petal veiner, a former plus a few basic modelling tools.

1 Thinly roll out the flower paste and cut out four petals per flower. Place the petals on a foam pad and stroke around the cut edges with a ball tool, half on the paste and half on the pad. Place a petal on top of one half of a double-sided veiner and cover with the second half, making sure it is lined up correctly. Press down firmly to emboss the petal.

2 Release the petal and place into a former. Vein the second petal and place opposite the first in the former. Vein two more petals and place these on top of the first two but at right angles.

3 Some red poppies have black markings – to add these, dust the base of each petal with black edible dust. Next cut small strips of paper towel, twist and insert between the petals to help give the petals movement and make them look more lifelike.

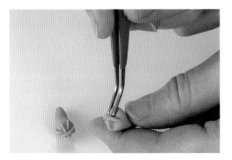

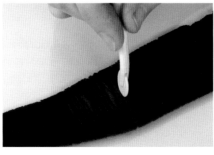

4 To create the flower centre, roll a ball of green flower paste into a cone shape, then using tweezers, pinch eight equal ridges into the top of the cone. Use a Dresden tool to mark light indentations down the cone.

5 To make the stamens, thinly roll out the black flower paste, then using a cutting wheel, make small strokes quickly backwards and forwards through the paste to create a narrow zigzagged cut.

6 Cut straight lines on either side of the zigzag to make two separate strips and wrap these around the flower centre. I added two layers to my poppy centre but you could add just one if desired.

Peony

Flamboyant and striking – the king of flowers – the peony is a wonderful bloom to use on cakes. Compared to many flowers, peonies have a considerable number of petals, however they can be made easily using just one cutter. To create a peony you will need flower paste in the colour of your choice, edible dust colours to complement the petal colour, a large five-petal blossom cutter, a ceramic veining tool, a foam pad, a ball tool and a polystyrene cup former, as well as the basic modelling tools, sugar glue and some paper towels.

1 Thinly roll out your flower paste and cut out two large five-petal blossoms. Take a cutting wheel and remove small 'V' sections of paste from the petal edges as shown. Cover the blossom you are not working on with plastic or a stay-fresh mat to prevent it drying out.

2 To give the petals some texture and interest, roll over each one with a ceramic veining tool. To do this, place the point of the tool in the centre of the flower and press down gently while rolling the tool in a radial movement across each petal.

3 Place the textured paste onto a foam pad and soften the edges with a ball tool. Hold the tool so it is half on the paste and half on the pad and stroke all the edges – the more pressure you apply the more movement you will give to the petals.

4 Place one set of petals in a polystyrene cup former then attach the second set of petals to the centre, arranging them so that they rest between the first set. Add space and movement between the petals by inserting small sections of twisted paper towel between the two layers.

Maroon Bloom
Putting a sugar peony on a cake gives it a delicate flourish, as seen on the Stacked Hatboxes cake in the Stencilling chapter.

5 To create the inside petals, cut five large blossoms from thinly rolled-out flower paste, cover all but one to prevent them drying out. Use the veiner and ball tool as before. Fold the edges of one petal in to the centre then fold again to create tightly curled petals. Add a little sugar glue if necessary but don't press the edges too tightly – you are not trying to stick the petals together, only to give them shape.

6 Repeat for the remaining petals then stand each one up so that they all sit at right angles to the central base of the original blossom.

7 Pinch the paste together at the base of the now vertical petals and place into the centre of the prepared outer petals, attaching with sugar glue. Repeat using the remaining four large blossoms.

8 Using a Dresden tool, open up and adjust the positioning of the petals to give a natural look. Take a dusting brush and add a little dust colour to the centre of some of the petals to add depth to the flower.

Pretty in Pink
Sugar peonies are versatile flowers that work in strong or delicate colours on a wide variety of designs.

9 Insert sections of twisted paper towel to help the petals stay in position while they dry. Allow the petals to harden but not completely. Remove the peony from its former – the petals should still have a little movement in them not be brittle and hard. Add a calyx, if required, then place in position on your cake. Add more paper towel if necessary and allow to dry thoroughly.

Embossing

If you want to add intricate or textured patterns to your cakes and cookies, then embossing the paste is probably the answer. Embossing is pressing a pattern into soft paste to leave a reversed image – transforming a plain surface into a beautifully crafted one. You can use commercially available embossers, cake-decorating tools or sugarcraft cutters, or you can make your own embossers depending on the effect you are trying to achieve. This chapter will inspire you to try a few different methods.

Chapter Contents:

Ready-Made Commercial Embossers

★ Small-scale embossers

★ Larger scale cutter-embossers

Textured Rolling Pins

Sugarcraft Cutters as Embossers

Tools as Embossers

★ Ball tool

★ Cutting wheel

★ Piping tubes (tips)

Using Non-Sugarcraft Items

★ Textured wallpaper

Making Your Own Embosser

Tip
Always emboss onto fresh paste – once paste has dried or crusted over the embosser will not work successfully.

Cushion Stack
Embossed modelling paste shapes have been used to add embellishments to the embossed sugarpaste covering these carved cushion cakes. See the Projects chapter for step-by-step instructions for this cake, plus the materials lists and instructions for all the other cakes and cookies shown in this chapter.

Ready-Made Commercial Embossers

On the following pages you will see that there are many ways of embossing soft paste, however often one of the easiest methods is to use commercially produced embossers. These are usually manufactured from food-grade plastics and have one patterned surface, often quite an intricate design, with a handle at the back to help lift the embosser off the textured paste. There is a huge range of embossers available, ranging from minute butterflies and elegant border patterns to life-sized flowers and stylish cake side designs – which you choose will obviously be determined by the cake or cookie you are planning to decorate.

Cutter-embossers

Stick embossers

Small-scale embossers

Choose your embosser wisely. You need to be able to hold the embosser firmly and securely in your hand. I find the stick embossers easy to use for small-scale designs.

Wedding Waistcoat
Embossing is a quick way to add interesting texture to your paste, as on this waistcoat design.

1 Roll out your sugarpaste to a thickness of 5mm (³⁄₁₆in), ideally using spacers, and either cover your cake or if you are covering a cookie leave the paste on your work surface. Hold your chosen embosser between your thumb and forefinger at right angles to the sugarpaste and press it into the soft paste. Repeat, ensuring that you apply the same pressure each time so that the pattern has an even depth.

2 If you are covering a cookie, cut out the shape from the embossed sugarpaste and transfer to the cookie.

Larger scale cutter-embossers

Many larger scale embossers have differing depths to their embossing edges, which means they can be used as both a cutter and an embosser. The following example shows this technique on a cupcake.

Blooming Gorgeous
The larger scale design on this cupcake was created using the embosser as a cutter too.

1 Roll out your sugarpaste to a thickness of 5mm (³⁄₁₆in), ideally using spacers, and stamp out a circle of paste to fit your cupcake. Choose a selection of appropriate cutter-embossers and emboss a pattern onto the soft sugarpaste. Don't worry if shapes overlap at this stage. Transfer the circle of sugarpaste onto a cupcake.

2 Thinly roll out your modelling paste – you will need to experiment to find the best thickness for the embosser you are using. The outside of the embosser should cut through the paste but the inside of the shape must remain intact. If you find it easier, cut out the shape with a craft knife. Cut out exactly the same shapes that you embossed onto your sugarpaste.

3 Transfer the embossed pieces to the embossed sugarpaste, sticking each shape over the corresponding shape on the sugarpaste, building up the pattern from the background to the foreground. Finally if desired, highlight the embossing by painting over the shapes with edible dusts or paste colours (see the Painting chapter).

Textured Rolling Pins

A textured rolling pin means that you can easily and speedily add an embossed pattern to a large area of sugarpaste. There are many different sizes and patterns available so chose one that suits your budget and design.

Conventional Use Roll out your sugarpaste or modelling paste, ideally using spacers. Remove the spacers and roll over your paste using your chosen textured rolling pin applying even pressure to give a regular pattern. Try not to re-roll as this can distort the pattern.

Experimental Use Don't be afraid to experiment, for example try over rolling different pins on the same piece of sugarpaste, try varying the pressure to give a textured wave effect or hold one end of the pin while rolling with the other to create a circular pattern.

Tender Roses
Every single piece of paste used on this cupcake has been subtly embossed using textured rolling pins.

Sugarcraft Cutters as Embossers

Many sugarcraft cutters work very well as embossers on sugarpaste, try experimenting with the ones that you have already. I personally think finer metal cutters are more effective than chunky cutters, however which you use really depends on the look you are after.

1 Roll out your sugarpaste to a thickness of 5mm (³⁄₁₆in), ideally using spacers and either cover your cake or if you are covering a cookie leave the paste on your work surface. Hold your chosen cutter at right angles to the sugarpaste and gently press it into the soft paste, taking care not to press it all the way through.

2 Repeat, ensuring that you apply the same amount of pressure each time so that the pattern has an even depth. If you are covering a cookie, cut out the shape from the embossed sugarpaste and transfer to the cookie.

Bridal Blooms
Small flower cutters were used to emboss the tiers of this wedding cake shaped cookie, and further texturing added for greater depth.

Tools as Embossers

Sugarcraft tools can be very effective when used to emboss soft paste. There are many suitable tools that can be used in lots of different ways, so take some time to experiment with those you already have in your toolbox. Here are three examples.

Ball tool

Try pressing the tool gently into soft paste to create a cup-shaped indent, always very attractive as it creates interesting shadows. Alternatively, try running your ball tool over the surface of the paste to create patterns, contours and ripples in the paste (see the Tools chapter).

Haute-Couture Heels
Using the ball tool to indent the petals of the flowers on this shoe cookie gives a 3D effect.

Wonderful Wellies
The line details on these welly boot cookies were embossed using a cutting wheel.

Cutting wheel

Rather that cutting through your paste to cut out shapes, apply less pressure and just indent the surface of the paste. This way you can make amazing patterns on your paste or add details to defined shapes.

Piping tubes (tips)

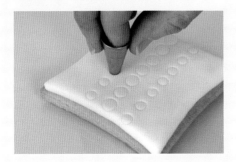

Try using the ends of different piping tubes (tips) to create patterns and impressions in the paste, here I am using a selection of round tubes, but closed star and petal tubes also are very effective.

Everything's Rosy
The spotty design on this cookie was made by embossing with the ends of different piping tubes (tips).

Tip

Allow yourself time to experiment – you never know what you might discover!

Using Non-Sugarcraft Items

There are many household items that you can use to emboss sugarpaste: spoon handles, buttons, bottle tops, brooches, pan scourers, stiff brushes, lace, wallpaper – in fact anything of a suitable size with a defined pattern on it, provided it is spotlessly clean or can be sealed with a food-grade product such as confectioners' glaze. See what you have in your cupboards!

Tip
Pan scourers are great for adding subtle texture to sugarpaste – it goes without saying to use only brand new ones!

Textured wallpaper

Most people don't think of wallpaper as an obvious choice for embossing sugarpaste, but it can work well provided that it is sealed first. Fashions in wallpapers change but there is currently a good selection of textured paper available that you can use, as shown below.

1 Select the wallpaper you wish to use, bearing in mind the scale of your work. I usually use this method on cake boards, which is what is shown, but there is nothing stopping you being more adventurous. Cut the paper to the size of the paste you wish to emboss and seal the textured surface with one or two coats of confectioners' glaze.

2 Cover your cake board with sugarpaste and trim to size. Place the paper on top of the soft paste and press down firmly in the centre with a smoother. Then, maintaining an even pressure, start to circle the smoother over the back of the paper to transfer the design.

3 Once complete, remove the paper and trim the paste where it has spread slightly over the edge of the board. Leave to dry.

Floral Elegance
The leaf design embossed onto the board of this mini-cake came from a sheet of textured wallpaper.

4 To accentuate the embossed design, if desired, mix a contrasting colour of sugarpaste with cooled boiled water until it is a spreadable consistency. Spread this over the board with a palette knife or side scrapper then remove the excess using a damp paper towel. Allow to dry.

Making Your Own Embosser

Sometimes, it is just not possible to find the right embosser so why not use your flair and originality to make your very own design? To do this you will need a design, a piece of acrylic that has been washed and sterilized with boiling water, royal icing, a piping (pastry) bag and a fine piping tube (tip) e.g. PME no. 1.

Tip

Embossed patterns made this way also work very well as a base for brushwork embroidery (see the Piping chapter).

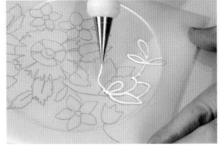
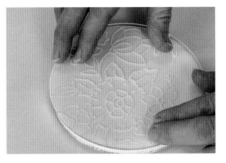

1 Draw or adapt your design as necessary. Remember that you will be creating a reversed image, so if your design needs to be a particular way round, flip your original image at this stage. For this example, I photographed an embroidered tablecloth and resized the resulting image so that it sits attractively on the board. I also traced the design so the outlines of the shapes are clearer.

2 Place the acrylic over the design and secure it in place with tape or a few dots of royal icing. Place the piping tube (tip) in the piping (pastry) bag and half fill with fresh royal icing that has been paddled to a smooth consistency. Then pipe over the outline of the design (see the Piping chapter).

3 Allow the icing to dry overnight in a warm, dry place. Once dry, position the embosser centrally over a freshly covered board or cake and press down firmly and evenly.

4 Remove the embosser to reveal the embossed pattern. In the cake shown to the left, I have piped coloured lines of royal icing over sections of the embossed pattern to recreate my embroidered tablecloth.

Sewing Sensation
The embosser used to create the design on this cake board was made especially for the purpose.

Tools

Sugarcraft tools are essential pieces of kit for any cake decorator, whether beginner or expert. This chapter shows you how some of these specialist tools can be used very effectively. I have not included every tool on the market, nor have I include all my personal favourites, as some are very specialized, instead I have selected ones that I think you will find particularity useful when decorating your own cakes.

Chapter Contents:

Gaudi's Grandeur
The wavy lines on the sides of this Gaudi-inspired cake were created with the round disc of a sugar shaper. See the Projects chapter for step-by-step instructions for this cake, plus the materials lists and instructions for all the other cakes and cookies shown in this chapter.

Sugarcraft Tools

In my own toolbox, I have tools from quite a few different manufacturers, as I often I prefer a tool from one particular supplier over the others available, for whatever reason. Sometimes it is how the tool is held that suits me, sometimes the superior finish or feel of the tool is what I like and other times because a tool is exclusive. If you can borrow some tools to try out, so much the better; if not buy the best you can afford, as having the right tools can make everything so much easier!

Tip

Choose your tools wisely and be wary of cheap sets, as they can be a poor investment. Always buy professional sugarcraft tools from reputable manufacturers.

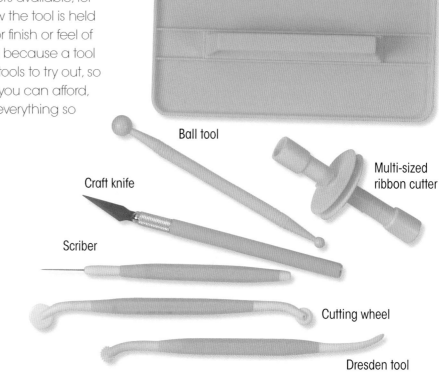

Cake smoother

Ball tool

Multi-sized ribbon cutter

Craft knife

Scriber

Cutting wheel

Dresden tool

Dresden Tool

This is probably the most-used tool in my toolbox! It has many uses – here are just a couple you may not have thought of.

Indenting a border trim

I often use a Dresden tool in conjunction with a sugar shaper to create a textured trim around my cakes. Following the instructions overleaf, create a length of paste using one of the round discs and attach to your cake. Take the Dresden tool and repeatedly press the sharper end into the paste to create a pattern.

Indenting fabric folds

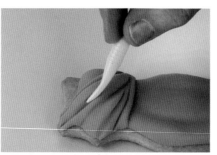

I find this a very useful technique. Cover your cake or cookie with soft sugarpaste then stroke the Dresden tool repeatedly through the paste, alternating the ends to create different effects. Keep the strokes close together so that the overall effect represents ruched or gathered fabric.

Glamorous Gown
The lifelike fabric drapes and folds on this dress cookie were created with a Dresden tool.

Ball Tool

One of the essential tools, a ball tool has two balls of differing sizes, one at either end. The tool is available in a number of different sizes, which you choose will depend on the scale of your work, but I suggest you start with the basic 6mm (¼in) and 12mm (½in) diameter balls.

Peachy Petals
The petals and leaves on this mini-cake were shaped with the ball tool.

Adding contours

Roll out soft sugarpaste and use to cover a cake board, cake or cookie. Make indentations in the soft paste by pressing the tool into the surface. Either remove the tool to leave a cupped imprint or gently run the tool over the paste to add contours and definition.

Softening petals/leaves

When you use cutters to cut out leaves and petals, there is always a sharp cut edge so a ball tool is used to soften this. Place your leaf or petal onto a foam pad. Take the ball tool and stroke around the edges, pressing the tool half on the paste and half on the pad.

Cupping paste

A ball tool can be used to turn a two-dimensional shape into a three-dimensional one. Thinly roll out some modelling paste and cut out a shape, for example a flower. Place on a foam pad. Press a ball tool into the centre of one petal and stroke along the paste towards the centre – the paste should curl in the direction that you have stroked.

Sugar Shaper

This is a fantastic tool – also often known as a clay gun, sugarcraft gun or craft gun – and is one that no cake decorator should be without. The patented pump action of the sugar shaper gives mechanical assistance to squeeze out pastes in various shapes and sizes. Most sugar mediums can be used with the sugar shaper, but the best results are obtained with modelling paste and pastillage. Sugarpaste can be used with the larger holed and mesh discs, but often gives ragged edges.

The discs and their uses

The sugar shaper includes 16 discs, which allow you to create ribbons, letters, frames, bricks, baskets, vines, grass, ropes and so on.

★ Use the mesh discs for hair, grass and flower stamens.

★ Use the slotted discs for ribbons, lattice and basketweave.

★ Use the cloverleaf-shaped disc for ropes.

★ Use the square and half-round discs for bricks and logs.

Tubes as discs

Try using PME piping tubes (tips) as an alternative to the sugar shaper discs, as they fit perfectly inside the shaper. I often use a number 1 or 1.5 when I want a smaller hole than the small round disc. The secret is to make sure the paste is very soft.

1 Firstly, add a little white vegetable fat (shortening) to the paste to stop it getting too sticky (but note that if too much is added the paste will not harden). Then dunk the paste into a container of cooled boiled water and knead to incorporate. Repeat until the paste feels soft and stretchy.

2 Insert the softened paste into the barrel of the sugar shaper, then add a disc and reassemble the tool.

Tip

The smaller the hole in the disc the softer the paste needs to be – think of chewed chewing gum and you won't go far wrong.

3 Push the plunger down to expel the air and pump the handle to build up pressure, until it 'bites'. The paste should squeeze out easily and smoothly – if it does not the consistency is probably incorrect so remove the paste and add some more fat (shortening) and/or water.

Round discs

These are probably the most versatile of all the discs. They can be used to add trim and many types of decoration. If you use pastillage, you can also create freestanding pieces of sugar work such as curls and spirals to pop into your cupcakes or add height to your cakes. Here are some ideas to try.

tip

Make sure the paste is really soft. All sugar media, with the exception of marzipan, will need softening by adding white vegetable fat (shortening) and cooled boiled water.

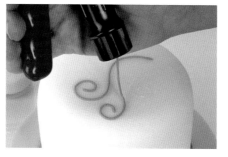

Idea 1 Soften some modelling paste and insert it into the sugar shaper together with a round disc. Squeeze out some of the paste and use directly as trim on cakes or cookies. I often use this technique to cover the join between a cake and its board, as it is a lot faster than most other options and looks very effective.

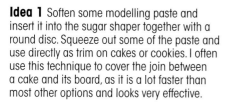

Idea 2 Many people find piping tricky so using a sugar shaper instead is a good solution. Take a fine paintbrush and paint your chosen pattern onto your cake or cookie with sugar glue. Squeeze out a length of paste and place it over the glue. Adjust the shape with a finger and/or a paintbrush as necessary. Cut the paste length to size. This technique works very well on the sides of cakes too.

Idea 3 Sometimes rather than adding the squeezed-out paste directly to a glued outline on a cake, it is easier to lay the paste on a non-stick surface to dry partially before attaching it. This enables you to use templates to shape your paste. Once the paste can be lifted without distorting, it can be glued in place. The wavy lines on the sides of the main cake for this chapter were created like this.

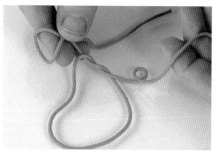

Idea 4 Another idea is to squeeze out paste onto your work surface and let it fractionally dry, to enable it to be handled more readily. The paste can now be used in much the same way as ribbon to tie a bow, make curls and so on.

Hot Pink Heels
The laces on this sexy shoe design were squeezed through the small round disc of a sugar shaper.

Mesh discs

These are excellent for creating hair, grass, flower centres, sheep's wool, tassels, and so on … the list is endless!

Fuzzy Flowers
Have fun experimenting with the mesh discs – these furry flowers are a break from the norm but look so effective!

Short Lengths Soften some modelling paste (as previously described) and insert into the sugar shaper fitted with one of the mesh discs. Squeeze out a small amount of the paste and use a Dresden tool to remove small tufts then add these directly to your cake or cookie.

Longer Lengths Begin as for short lengths but continue squeezing out the paste to the required length then remove with a Dresden tool. If making a tassel, pinch the cut ends together; if creating hair, remove a few strands at a time and attach as required.

Teatime Treat
Rope can be used in a myriad of designs and is the perfect finishing touch on this teapot cookie.

Rope disc

This disc looks like a cloverleaf.

To create a rope, squeeze out a length of paste then carefully twist.

Love twisting? Try this…

★ Make a multi-coloured rope by twisting together three lengths of different coloured paste made by one of the round discs.

★ Try twisting lengths of some of the other shapes too such as the square or ribbon.

Multi-Sized Ribbon Cutter

This tool is a great time saver as it enables you to cut strips the same size, easily and quickly. The beauty of this tool is that the cutting wheels can be set to cut strips between 3.5mm (⅛in) and 54mm (2⅛in) wide, allowing you to create fine ribbons as well as wide strips.

Café Crème
Ribbons can be used to create a wide range of embellishments, including the exquisite bow on this sophisticated cupcake.

1 Assemble your tool so that the cutting wheels are set to the required width. Thinly roll out some modelling paste. Holding the handles of the tool in either hand, firmly and evenly roll the cutting edges of the tool through the paste.

2 You should be left with a beautifully cut ribbon. If the tool hasn't cut cleanly through all the paste, perhaps due to uneven pressure, run a craft knife along the edges to tidy it up. Leave the paste to firm up for a moment or two then pick it up and use as desired.

Tip
Experiment with the ribbon cutter's wavy and stitching wheels – strips cut with one straight and one wavy edge are great for trimming the join between a cake and its board.

Cutting Wheel

This is a very useful tool, which is most frequently used to cut modelling paste freehand. The advantage of using a cutting wheel is that it slightly curves the top cut edge of the paste, so shapes appear softer. A cutting wheel can also be used to add texture to paste.

Kitten Heels
The animal print decoration on this chic shoe was cut freehand from modelling paste with a cutting wheel.

Cutting freehand shapes   ## Creating feathering

Roll out your modelling paste between narrow spacers, ideally on a non-stick work board. Select either the small or large wheel and hold the tool in your hand like a pencil. Roll the wheel across the paste, pressing down with enough pressure to make a clean cut. Remove the excess paste from around the shape. Allow the shape to firm up for a moment or two then transfer to your covered cake or cookie.

Thinly roll out some modelling paste then run the tool, using small strokes, quickly backwards and forwards over the paste to create a feathered appearance. Use as it is or cut into a strip and coil to make a flower centre, as used on the Perfect Poppies cake the Painting chapter.

Tip
A cutting wheel can also be run repeatedly through sugarpaste to give it a textured appearance.

Craft Knife

A craft knife is a very useful tool, as its sharp pointed blade means that it can cut intricate details easily and large shapes cleanly. Handle with care and always cut onto a surface that will not mark or be damaged by the blade. I use a Corian work board and highly rate them, but they are expensive and other options are available. For best results use thinly rolled modelling paste. I usually recommend that your paste be 1.5mm (¹⁄₁₆in) thick and that you use spacers to help you achieve an even thickness, however sometimes a design calls for thinner paste and other times a chunkier look is more appropriate. Here are some examples of ways you can use a craft knife, but don't be afraid to experiment to see how you can use this versatile tool.

Sunburst Stripes
The funky stripes on this mini-cake were all cut with a craft knife.

Cutting basic shapes

Roll out your modelling paste between narrow spacers. Hold your knife securely and cut out your required shape, using a template if required. In this example I have used a craft knife and a straight edge to cut even strips.

Cutting to shape in situ

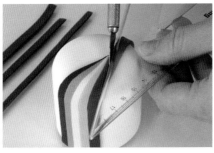

A craft knife is an excellent tool for fine-tuning paste shapes that you have already attached to your cake, as its sharp blade means you can cut away sections without applying any pressure to the surface of the covered cake.

Cutting intricate shapes

A craft knife is the best tool for cutting intricate shapes. The thin blade means that it is possible to cut out fine details, such as on this silhouette. An intricate shape will need turning as you cut so make sure this is possible, also you will get a better result if you make a negative template so that you press down on the area around the shape not on the required shape itself.

Slick Silhouette
Use your craft knife to create complex cut outs, such as this silhouette from the Patchwork Heart cake in the Colour chapter.

Tip
Change the blade of your craft knife regularly to ensure crisp cuts every time.

Non-Sugarcraft Tools

The craft world is full of interesting tools, so next time you are in a craft shop or browsing online, see what you can find that will transfer easily to sugarcraft – just make sure that the tools can be cleaned or sterilized and be wary of plastics that have not been approved for food use. Here's how you can use paper punches to great effect.

1 Thinly roll out your modelling paste between narrow spacers, you may need to make your paste slightly firmer and thinner than usual. Allow the paste to harden for a few minutes then slot the paste into the punch.

2 Press down firmly on the punch and then release. Carefully slide the paste out of the punch. You can use both the punched-out sections of paste and the pattern that has been cut into the original paste. Leave the delicate cut paste to firm up a little before attaching to your cake or cookie.

Using gold leaf

Great results can also be achieved using a paper punch in combination with gold leaf. Thinly roll out your modelling paste on white vegetable fat (shortening) and carefully place the paste fat side down onto the gold leaf. Press gently over the paste to help bond the two materials together. Turn the paste over and remove the backing paper from the gold. Allow the paste to firm up then insert into your punch and cut, as shown in step 2.

Tip
Choose your punch wisely – corner punches are not easy to use and punches that emboss as well as cut tend not to be as successful on sugar.

Pleased as Punch
This unusual filigree-style design was created using a general craft punch.

Piping

Piped details can turn a simple design into a stunning cake and yet many people shy away from even trying their hand at piping. This chapter will help demystify the art and inspire you to perfect the technique. The basics are not difficult to master – having the correct equipment and icing consistency is key, whether it's buttercream or royal icing. Then all you need is practice to become familiar with the amounts of pressure required as you pipe.

Chapter Contents:

Tip
The techniques for piping buttercream and royal icing are the same – it is the scale that is different. If you wish to pipe a small rose rather than a large buttercream one, simply use a smaller petal tube (tip) and royal icing instead.

Coral Creation
Piping results in a wealth of different effects – brushwork embroidery and piped dots feature on this amazing tiered creation. See the Projects chapter for step-by-step instructions for this cake, plus the materials lists and instructions for all the other cakes and cookies shown in this chapter.

Equipment

Whether you opt to pipe using buttercream or royal icing, to get started you will need some basic equipment.

Piping tubes (tips)

Also known as nozzles and pipes, there are many piping tubes to choose from and which shape and size you select will depend on the medium you are using and the design of the piping you wish to create. Generally, however, the tubes used for buttercream tend to be much larger than those used for delicate royal iced details.

Tubes are manufactured from either plastics or metals such as nickel-plated brass and stainless steel. For best results, always use professional piping tubes and avoid ones with seams. If your budget allows, use stainless steel tubes where possible, as these do not rust or break and should last you a lifetime. Also be aware that the number series used to identify piping tubes is not standardized so you'll find that each manufacturer has its own slightly different numbering system. For example a Wilton no. 10 equals a PME no. 16. Before using a tube, always ensure that it is thoroughly clean and dry, especially when using the very small ones.

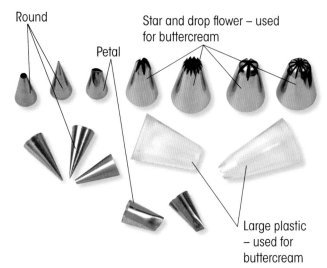

Round

Petal

Star and drop flower – used for buttercream

Large plastic – used for buttercream

Piping bag couplers

These clever devices are wonderful time savers; they are added into the end of piping (pastry) bags to enable tubes (tips) to be easily changed, thus removing the need to have a new piping bag for each tube.

Piping (pastry) bags

These are available in two main types: reusable bags, now usually manufactured from proofed nylon rather than traditional cotton, which required boiling to sterilize, and disposable bags manufactured from clear plastic or greaseproof paper. I personally favour large plastic disposable bags for piping buttercream and small proofed nylon reusable bags for royal icing, however it is important for you to find out which you prefer. Many people also like to make their own greaseproof paper bags – the choice is yours.

Tip

Look for piping (pastry) bags with closed ends as these allow you to trim the end of the bag to fit your particular piping tube (tip) or coupler.

Buttercream

Beautiful swirls of light and fluffy buttercream (see the Sugar Recipes section) are what many strive for but there are other options to try! It is important that your buttercream is the correct consistency and temperature. If it is too stiff and cold it will be very difficult to pipe successfully so you should re-beat it and add a little more water or milk. If it is too soft and warm it will not retain its shape, so chill it to cool it down then, if necessary, add a little more icing (confectioners') sugar and re-beat.

Rose Swirls
Practice makes perfect – continue piping your buttercream swirls until you achieve seamless roses like these.

Swirls

To pipe swirls you will need a large star or drop flower tube (tip). I suggest you try experimenting with different piping tubes, as you will achieve different effects with quite similar looking tubes.

1 Place your chosen tube (tip) into a large piping (pastry) bag then half fill the bag with buttercream. Twist the top of the bag to seal it. Hold the bag vertically slightly above the centre of the cupcake.

2 Apply pressure to the bag, then move the tube to the edge of the cake and go around the centre in an anticlockwise (counter-clockwise) direction, holding the tube above the cake surface so the icing falls into place.

3 To create a simple rose as shown in this example, release the pressure and remove the piping bag when you have completed one full circle.

Variation Alternatively continue piping by adding one or two smaller circles of buttercream on top of the first.

Tip

Once you have mastered the basics, try adding two colours of buttercream into your piping (pastry) bag at the same time to give a striking two-tone effect.

Peaks

This technique works best with more rather than less points/petals on the piping tube (tip). So I suggest you try experimenting with large tubes with at least eight points/petals. Remember, different effects are created with quite similar looking tubes.

1 Place your chosen tube (tip) into a large piping (pastry) bag then half fill the bag with buttercream. Twist the top of the bag to seal it. Hold the bag vertically slightly above the centre of the cupcake. Keeping the bag still, apply continuous pressure and allow the icing to spread towards the edge of the cupcake.

2 Once the buttercream has spread, slowly start to lift the bag while maintaining an even pressure. Release the pressure once the desired height has been reached and remove the bag.

Variation 1 An alternative to the previous step is to rotate the cupcake in your hand while lifting the bag – this adds a subtle twist to the pattern in the icing.

Variation 2 Alternatively, rather than piping one large peak, use the same tube to pipe lots of small stars/flowers by applying pressure for only a short time before removing the tube.

Peak of Perfection
Peaks of piped buttercream make the ideal basis for these cupcakes topped with small moulded flowers and a red pastillage rope-effect flourish.

Daisies

This is a very pretty technique that quickly transforms a cupcake. The technique works well with a range of petal and leaf tubes (tips), so experiment to find the tubes you like and those that suit the scale of your cake.

1 Place your chosen petal or leaf tube (tip) into a large piping (pastry) bag and half fill with buttercream. Twist the top of the bag to seal it. Starting at the centre of a cupcake, hold the bag so the thick section of the tube is pointing inwards and the thin section outwards. Start squeezing the bag and draw it out towards the edge then back in to the centre of the cake.

2 Repeat, using even pressure for each petal, turning the cupcake in your hand as you pipe.

3 Add a second layer, making the petals shorter and then, if desired, add a third or fourth layer. How many layers you chose to add will be determined by the size of your cupcake and the size of your tube.

Divine Daisies
These beautiful piped daisies need nothing more than a ball of sugarpaste in the centre to complete the look.

Tip
If your buttercream gets too warm and starts to melt as it comes out of the tube (tip), place the bag in the fridge for five minutes.

Roses

Classic roses are always popular. They have been piped in royal icing for centuries however the technique works just as well in buttercream. Choose a petal tube (tip) of a suitable size – these are available from tiny through to massive, I suggest you opt for one about 1cm (⅜in) long. To enable you to turn your rose quickly while piping, you will also require an icing nail.

Vintage Roses
A full rose bloom makes the ultimate cupcake decoration and is delicious in piped buttercream.

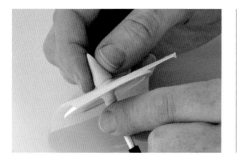

1 Cut small squares of cellophane or waxed paper and attach one to the top of your icing nail with a little buttercream. The first step is to make a cone of a suitable size – you can pipe this with buttercream but I have found that making cones from sugarpaste gives a firmer centre to the roses. Attach or pipe a cone to the centre of the icing nail.

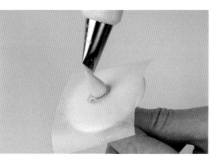

2 Place your chosen petal tube (tip) into a large piping (pastry) bag and half fill with buttercream. Position the tube at right angles to the nail with the wider end of the tube at the bottom and the thinner end at the top. Raise the tube up so that the tip of the cone is halfway up the tube. You are now ready to start piping.

3 Start squeezing the bag, turning the nail as you pipe to create the tight coiled centre of the rose, about one and a half times around.

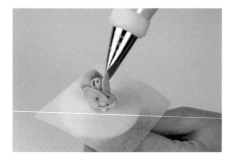

4 Keeping the nail upright, add three interlocking petals around the centre. Start at the base of the cone and apply pressure to the bag, lifting the tube up to the top of the centre and then drop back to the base to create the first petal. Pipe two more to complete the circle.

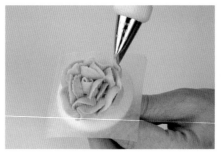

5 Add the next row of rose petals, making these more open by tilting the nail not the tube, this time adding five petals in the row. Continue adding as many rows of petals as desired, increasing the number of petals in each row by two each time.

6 Slip the cellophane or waxed paper square from the nail and leave the piped rose to dry. Once the rose has dried sufficiently to be handled, carefully remove the protective square and add the rose to the top of the cupcake or cake.

Royal Icing

Royal icing (see the Sugar Recipes section) is seen by many as old fashioned, however I would argue that simple pressure-piped royal iced details and accents can complement contemporary cake design beautifully. On the following pages I have selected a number of royal icing piping techniques that I believe you will find very useful.

Piping with royal icing

The most important thing with royal icing is that the consistency of the icing is correct for the technique you wish to use. For the techniques that follow you will need both soft peak (normal) and smooth icing.

★ **Soft peak (normal) royal icing:** After beating your royal icing, make peaks in the icing with a palette knife and if the tips of the peaks bend over the consistency is correct, if not re-beat until the correct consistency is achieved. This icing is used for drop line work.

★ **Smooth royal icing:** Paddle some soft peak icing on a non-stick board using the flat lower surface of palette knife to expel all the air bubbles. Then if necessary add a few drops of cooled boiled water to give a perfectly smooth icing. This icing is used for piping small shapes and for brushwork embroidery.

Dots

It is essential with this technique that your icing is of the correct consistency – you want to pipe dots or pearls not pointed cones. The smaller the hole in your tube (tip) the more critical this is.

Whole Lotta Dots
Royal iced dots are easy, effective and versatile decorations on a myriad of designs.

1 Place a small round tube (tip), e.g. PME no. 1 or 2, into a small piping (pastry) bag and half fill with freshly paddled smooth royal icing. Supporting your hand, either on your work surface or turntable, or with your other hand, hold the tube fractionally above the surface on which you wish to pipe.

2 Squeeze the bag until the dot is the required size, release the pressure and only then remove the tube – this helps avoid any unwanted peaks. Remember: squeeze, release and lift.

Tip
Fresh icing is always better than old icing for piping as it holds its shape, is stiffer and is therefore easier to control.

Hearts

These are a simple variation on dots. For best results use freshly paddled, smooth royal icing.

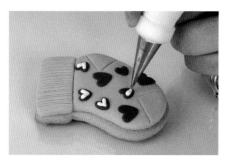

1 Pipe a dot using smooth royal icing, but rather than removing the tube (tip), pull it through the centre of the dot to create a teardrop shape before removing.

2 Pipe a second dot close to the top of the first teardrop, then pull the tube through the centre to meet the narrow end of the first teardrop to create a heart shape.

Baby Booties
Piping hearts on top of sugarpaste hearts creates a charming layered effect.

Drop line work

This technique involves dropping lines of icing onto the cake surface – it takes a little practice but I think it's worth it. I have found this technique an excellent way of representing contemporary lace work on cakes.

Tip

To avoid lines breaking, don't use your bag for more than 15–20 minutes, as your hands will make the icing too warm. Always re-beat your icing before starting again.

Lovely Lace
Drop line work was used to link the floral motifs of this mini-cake, transforming it into a lace-effect design.

1 Place a small round tube (tip), e.g. PME no. 1, into a small piping (pastry) bag and half fill with freshly beaten soft peak royal icing. Hold the bag with your forefinger pointing down the front ready to apply pressure with only your thumb.

2 Touch the surface where your line is to start with the tip of the tube and at the same time lightly apply pressure to the bag. As the icing starts to come out, lift the tube up from the cake so it is at least 4cm (1½in) above the sugarpaste surface.

3 When the icing is of the length you need, release the pressure and place the icing down onto the surface of the cake. Remember: touch, lift and place.

Brushwork embroidery

This is a technique I learned many years ago but have always loved. It is basically a piped outline that is faded into the sugarpaste surface. For the most striking effects, choose either dark sugarpaste and light icing or the converse. Your royal icing should be of a smooth consistency.

1 The first stage is to emboss or scribe a design onto your cake or cookie. The quickest method is to use a ready-made embosser on soft sugarpaste. However, if you wish to create a unique design, either make your own embosser (see the Embossing chapter) and use on soft sugarpaste or scribe your chosen design onto your cake (once the sugarpaste has set) with a scriber needle.

2 Place a suitable small round piping tube (tip), e.g. PME no. 1.5 or 2, into a piping (pastry) bag and half fill with freshly prepared smooth royal icing. Which size tube you require will depend on how heavily your design is embossed. For most shapes you need to work from the background to the foreground, so choose a small section at the back of your design and pipe around the outer section only.

3 Dampen a reasonably firm brush of a suitable size with cooled boiled water, blotting off any excess moisture with a paper towel. Place the brush on the wet icing and draw the icing towards the centre of the design with long strokes to give the design a natural feel.

4 When brushing through the icing, aim to keep the outer line unbroken, but you can always add more icing if necessary. Continue working around your design, brushing each section as soon as you have piped it to prevent the icing drying out.

Tip
While you are perfecting this technique, add a little piping gel to the royal icing to slow down the drying process, giving you more time to work on your design.

Monochrome Mugs
A damp brush is all that's needed to turn a piped design into a brushwork embroidery masterpiece.

Moulds

If you want to make beautiful sugar decorations but do not have much time, one of the best solutions is to choose a silicone mould. This chapter covers the basics of moulding using a single colour and then shows you what can be achieved by introducing more colours. It also shows you how to use double-sided veiners to create lifelike leaves, and closes with ways to make your own unique moulds.

Chapter Contents:

Silicone Moulds

Single-Colour Moulding

★ The pastes to use

Two-Colour Moulding

Complex Shapes

Double-Sided Veiners

Making Your Own Moulds

★ Using pastillage

★ Using moulding gel

★ Creating moulds from scratch using moulding gel

Tip
There are various types of moulds for sugarcraft but the examples in this chapter use silicone moulds, which are the most widely available and are highly affordable.

Prettiest Posy
The roses, chrysanthemums and smaller blossoms decorating this ball cake were all created relatively quickly using moulds. See the Projects chapter for step-by-step instructions for this cake, plus the materials lists and instructions for all the other cakes and cookies shown in this chapter.

Silicone Moulds

There are literally thousands of different food-grade silicone moulds available, so take the time to look around and find ones that you like and that are a suitable size for the designs you are planning. All silicone moulds are soft and flexible but their quality does vary. Lower-quality moulds are more prone to tearing, while higher-quality moulds can withstand high fluctuations in temperature, are odourless and completely non-stick.

All moulds need to be treated with respect. When removing a design, be careful not to overstretch the sides of the mould. Silicone moulds can be washed with soap and water but they can also be placed on the top rack of a dishwasher. To dry the moulds, shake out the excess water and allow to air dry. Do not attempt to towel dry a silicone mould as it will pick up large quantities of lint from the cloth.

Single-Colour Moulding

The most straightforward approach to moulding is to use just one colour of paste.

The pastes to use

Moulds are very simple to use provided you select the correct paste and it is of the right consistency for the mould you have chosen. The secret of success for many moulds is to use a firm paste. I favour modelling paste made with gum tragacanth rather than CMC (Tylose) (see the Sugar Recipes section), however for some highly detailed moulds with undercut sections the best approach is to use softer paste so that the mould is easier to fill completely and then to place the mould in the freezer for 15–30 minutes before releasing the design. Don't be afraid to experiment and try using other pastes such as marzipan with a little added gum for strength, flower paste and modelling chocolate.

Roses are Red…
Simple moulded roses and leaves made in single colours adorn these cupcakes, baked in pretty floral paper cases.

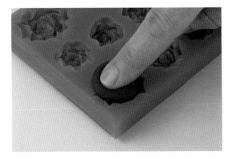

1 Knead a small amount of modelling paste to warm it, then roll a ball of paste slightly larger than the mould cavity. Place the ball of paste into the mould ensuring that the sugar surface being placed in the mould is perfectly smooth – if there are small joins visible they will probably be visible on your finished piece.

2 Push the paste into the mould firmly to ensure the deeper sections are filled. Then stroke the paste around the edges of the mould with your finger to help it fill the mould completely.

3 Remove the excess paste with a palette knife so that the back of the mould is flat. Note: a few moulds will need a slight dome otherwise they do not remain complete when de-moulded.

4 To remove the paste, carefully flex the mould to release.

Tip

If you are using a large or intricate mould it may be easier to add the paste into the mould in sections, pressing down firmly after each addition.

Two-Colour Moulding

Flowers really lend themselves to being made from moulds, and adding a centre of a different colour brings them to life. Here I have used a daisy mould but the technique can easily be adapted for other moulds.

Tip

If you are not getting enough detail, check that you are pressing the paste firmly and that your paste is not too stiff.

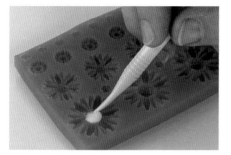

1 Knead a small amount of modelling paste to warm it, then roll a ball of paste smaller than the centre of the flower mould. Press the ball into the centre of the mould – ideally the paste should just line this section so that when the next colour is added it doesn't spread into the surrounding area. If necessary, define the edge of the shape using the pointed end of a Dresden tool.

2 Roll a ball of paste slightly larger than the mould cavity. Place the ball of paste into the mould ensuring that the sugar surface being placed into the mould is perfectly smooth. Push the paste into the mould firmly.

3 Remove the excess paste with a palette knife so that the back of the mould is flat. Then, using a Dresden tool, make sure that each petal is properly defined by drawing the excess paste between petals into the centre.

4 To remove the paste, carefully flex the mould to release. If the coloured centre of the flower has spread to the surrounding petals, you need to add less paste into the centre next time.

Flowery Flip-Flops
A moulded daisy is the focal point on these fun cookies, which complements the embossed surface design.

Complex Shapes

The secret when moulding with a number of colours is to use just the right amount of each colour – I suggest you have a few trial runs to work this out. Practice runs can also help you choose the order in which you add the colours – usually it is best to fill the deepest recesses of the mould first, but you will need to experiment with the mould you are using. For the example here, it is the gold disc and purple coil that need to be added first – they are the sections of the moulded face that are the smallest and most detailed.

Masked Marvel
This design is moulded then painted to become an authentic-looking Venetian mask.

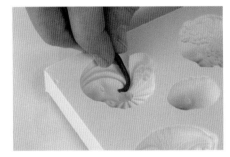

1 Press a small ball of paste into the centre of the mould – ideally the paste should just line this section. Roll a thin sausage of purple paste and press it in position, remove most of the paste just leaving the tip of the coil. If you do not trim the paste at this stage you'll probably find that once de-moulded the purple paste will spread into the face.

2 Roll a ball of white modelling paste slightly larger than the face and press into the face section. Use a Dresden tool to shape and mould the paste into the appropriate section of the mould.

3 Add some aqua modelling paste to one side of the mould, ensuring that it fits snugly and doesn't overlap a different section. Use a Dresden tool to help you achieve clean lines between the shapes.

4 Roll some navy blue paste into a cone and add to the top section. Fill the remainder of the mould with purple paste and press down firmly to ensure the mould is tightly filled.

5 Remove the excess paste with a palette knife so that the back of the mould is flat. Carefully flex the mould to release. Achieving perfect results each time takes a little practice, so don't be disappointed if the first time you try the colours have spread.

Double-Sided Veiners

Silicone veiners are an excellent way of adding lifelike edible leaves and petals to your cakes. There are hundreds of petal and leaf veiners to try, ranging from the ever-popular rose, to familiar woodland tree leaves and exotic orchids. Remember, you do not always need to be botanically correct; many leaves and petals are similar to others so one veiner can be used to produce a range of different petals or leaves. The best paste to use in a double-sized veiner is flower paste (see the Sugar Recipes section), however a firm modelling paste can work just as well, although the resulting leaves or petals are less robust.

Tip
Try to arrange the leaves on your cake while there is still some flexibility in the paste – once they are dry they are very brittle and can be difficult to arrange.

1 Smear white vegetable fat (shortening) over your work board to stop the paste sticking, then thinly roll out some golden brown flower paste or firm modelling paste and cut out leaves using leaf cutters of an appropriate size. Place a sheet of clear plastic or a stay-fresh mat over the shapes until they are required to prevent them drying out.

2 Place a few leaves on a foam pad. Take the ball tool and stroke around the edges of the paste by pressing the tool half on the paste and half on the pad to soften the cut edge (see the Tools chapter).

3 Next, place a leaf in an appropriate double-sided veiner, press down hard on the top of the veiner and then release and remove the veined leaf. You will be able to see at this point if your original paste was the correct thickness – if the leaf looks a bit fleshy then the paste was too thick; if the leaf has fallen apart then the paste was probably too thin.

4 Place the veined leaves onto dimpled foam, formers or scrunched up paper towel and allow to partially dry in a natural shape.

5 Use edible dusts to colour the leaves. Take a dry dusting brush, dip the tip of the brush into burgundy dust, tap off the excess and dust some of the leaf edges. Next, add other colours to the central areas of the leaves to give a natural look. Set the dusts by very carefully passing the leaves through steam to intensify their colours.

Falling Leaves
Double-sided veiners can create realistic leaves in minutes. Why not create your own autumnal cake?

Making Your Own Moulds

It can be very rewarding and cost effective to make your own moulds – not every attempt will be a triumph but you'll have a lot of fun experimenting and you'll be very proud of your successes. As well as making moulds from pastillage, there are a number of specialist products available to sugarcrafters for making moulds – my favourite is called moulding gel and as can be seen on the following pages, it is easy and quick to use and best of all can be reused again and again.

Christmas Crackers
Wallpaper and lace make a great basis for pastillage moulds, which is how these festive cookies came into being.

Using pastillage

Pastillage is a paste made from sugar that sets very hard and is less prone to moisture attack than other pastes (see the Sugar Recipes section). These properties mean that it is the most appropriate paste from which to make a reusable mould.

1 The first step is to choose an object to make into a mould, ideally for this method the object needs to be flat but textured; I find lace and textured wallpaper ideal candidates, but I am sure you can find many other objects to use.

2 Sterilize the object or, if more appropriate, add a food-grade barrier. If you are using wallpaper, seal the side you are using by painting over the pattern with one or two coats of confectioners' glaze.

3 Thickly roll out some pastillage onto a hardboard cake board. Working quickly to avoid the pastillage crusting over, place the sealed wallpaper onto the paste and roll over it firmly with a rolling pin or smoother. Remove the paper and place the textured pastillage in a warm dry place to dry completely. This may take a few days, so be patient.

4 Once the pastillage mould is thoroughly dry, roll out some sugarpaste on white vegetable fat (shortening) and place the paste fat side down over the pastillage – this helps prevent the paste sticking to the dried mould.

5 Press down on the paste with a smoother to transfer the pattern – you may need to experiment with the amount of pressure required but try not to exert too much pressure as this may cause the mould to break.

6 Carefully remove the sugarpaste, which is now textured with a raised pattern, from the mould and use to decorate cakes and cookies. Store the mould away from moisture and it can be used repeatedly.

Using moulding gel

This product is specially formulated for the cake-decorating industry, it is food safe and completely harmless if accidentally ingested. The beauty of this product is that it is so easy to use and can simply be melted and used again once a mould is no longer needed or if it is not successful. Always work on spotlessly clean surfaces to prevent the gel picking up foreign bodies, which may reduce its effectiveness, and do not allow the gel to come into contact with water – don't be tempted to wash your moulds! The simplest way to make a mould is to find a suitable object to use. Try using buttons, jewellery, coins, children's toys, or shells, as I have done here.

She Sells Seashells...
These sugar seashells look so realistic because they were moulded from real life shells.

1 First. you need to find a suitable container in which to pour the gel. There are various options: try rolling out some modelling clay, not too thinly, place the object in the centre then bring up the sides and pinch together to form a container; alternatively make a container from aluminium foil or use a plastic beaker or small bowl.

2 Melt the gel following the instructions that come with the product, and then pour into the container until the model is completely covered. Gently tap the container onto your work surface to encourage any trapped air bubbles to rise to the surface.

3 Leave until the gel is set – for small moulds this is often only 5–10 minutes, however to speed up the process place the mould in the freezer until the gel has cooled. Once set carefully peel away the container and remove the object from the mould. If any gel has flooded under the object, trim this off with a craft knife before releasing.

4 Knead some modelling paste to warm it up and roll it into a ball. Press the ball firmly into the newly created mould.

5 Level the paste with the top of the mould with a palette knife and then carefully release. If your moulded shape is a success, repeat; if not then simply re-melt the gel and try again.

6 Once the moulded shapes are dry, dilute some paste colours in clear alcohol then paint as appropriate (see the Painting chapter).

Creating moulds from scratch using moulding gel

This method allows you to reproduce an object easily that you have modelled just once – a great time saver when you have a large batch of cupcakes to decorate. To create your own shape to mould you will need some non-toxic modelling clay (such as Plasticine) available from toy and art shops plus a few basic modelling tools. You will also need to decide on a subject to be modelled. Do your research and choose something appropriate. For the example here, I have chosen a teapot but many other three-dimensional objects would work just as well.

Tea and Cake
Creating a bespoke design on a whole batch of cookies or cupcakes is very time consuming, unless you make a mould.

1 Collect images of the subjects you wish to model and resize these using a computer or photocopier. Choose one to use. As my mould is to be used on cupcakes, I have drawn circles around my collected images to help me see which design of teapot looks the most attractive in this shape.

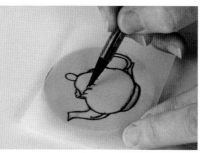

2 Using tracing paper and a soft pencil, draw around the outline and distinguishing features of the image. Remove the tracing paper, turn it over and draw over all the lines again, unless of course you are happy with a mirror image. Roll out some non-toxic modelling clay and place the traced shape the correct way up on top. Transfer the design to the clay by going over the lines with a pencil a final time.

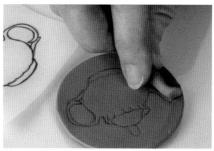

3 Remove the tracing paper – you are now ready to start creating the model. When deciding where to start, look carefully at your image – you want to add all the sections that are furthest away first and finish with those closest to you. I am starting with the spout and handle, following this with the lid and then the body.

4 Using the tracing as a guide, add small sections of clay at a time, moulding and blending the clay with your fingers and modelling tools as appropriate. Unlike sugar, sections of modelling clay can be blended so that no joins are visible.

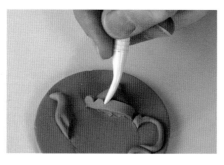

5 Details can be added to your model using modelling tools and embossers. Here I am using a Dresden tool to add the teapot's shaped rim detail. The roses on the body of the teapot are made using small embossed shapes (see the Embossing chapter).

6 Once your model is complete, add strips of modelling clay around the model to make a container. Melt the gel and pour over the model to cover completely. Once set, carefully peel away the container and model from the mould. Your mould is now ready to use.

Cake Jewellery

Cake jewellery adds a touch of sparkle and luxury to cakes – use on its own or combined with sugar decorations to make eye-catching centrepieces. Creating cake jewellery pieces is thoroughly enjoyable. The beading world is seductive, all those wonderful colours, shapes, choices and possibilities. If you have never tried cake jewellery before, this chapter starts with some introductory techniques. If you feel inspired to make a cake crown, a number of useful techniques are included – just choose those that appeal most.

Chapter Contents:

Crowning Glory
Jewellery adds an extra dimension to cakes – the glamorous crown on this cake transforms it into an opulent design. See the Projects chapter for step-by-step instructions for this cake, plus the materials lists and instructions for all the other cakes shown in this chapter.

A Guide to Wires and Beads

Before rushing ahead into creating your first cake jewellery it is worthwhile reading the brief introduction that follows to familiarize yourself with the basics.

Essential tools and materials

Having the right tools and equipment always makes the job easier.

☆ **Wire cutters** – these are vital, as you don't want to ruin a good pair of scissors.

☆ **Jewellery pliers** – essential for creating fountains and some cake crown elements.

☆ **Round-nose pliers** – these are used to make coils, so are only necessary once you wish to experiment with these.

☆ **Bead mat** – these are a fantastic and relatively new invention, they stop your beads scattering because if you drop a bead the mat catches it rather than letting it roll.

☆ **Glue** – you will need a strong acrylic-based non-toxic jewellery glue, available from most bead and jewellery-making suppliers.

Wires

Many people find wires confusing so here I have split them into groups to help demystify them. It is very important that you use the right wire for the right purpose. Some of the wires are interchangeable, while others are not. There are two different parameters when choosing a wire:

☆ **The core material of the wire** – as this gives you an indication of its strength. For example, a steel-cored wire will be a lot stronger than a copper-cored wire of the same thickness.

☆ **The size or thickness of the wire** – i.e. the gauge or diameter.

Wires are measured both by gauge and diameter, however these measurements vary depending on where you live or where the wire was manufactured. In Europe, wire is measured in standard wire gauge (swg) and millimetres (mm) however in the United States, American wire gauge (Amg) and inches (in) are used.

☆ **Note: European gauges and metric diameters are used in the instructions throughout this chapter – to convert these, please refer to the conversion chart opposite.**

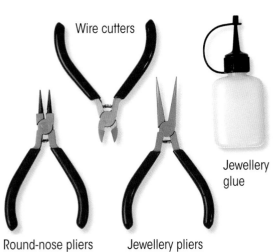

Wire cutters

Round-nose pliers

Jewellery pliers

Jewellery glue

Tip

All cake jewellery should be removed from a cake before it is cut. Never stick non-edible beads or crystals directly into the icing of a cake.

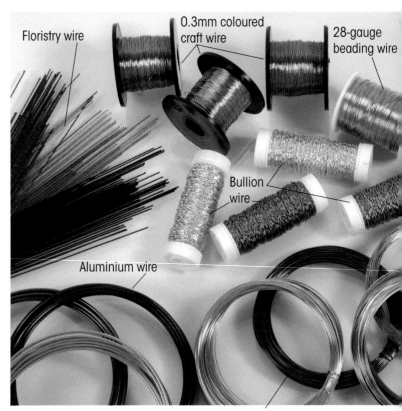

Floristry wire

0.3mm coloured craft wire

28-gauge beading wire

Bullion wire

Aluminium wire

0.5mm coloured craft wire

Wire gauge conversion chart

Wire	Metric (mm)	Standard wire gauge (swg)	American wire gauge (in)	
Soft beading/binding wires				
Bullion wire	0.315	28	0.012	Thin
0.3mm coloured craft wire	0.315	28	0.012	
28-gauge beading wire	0.315	28	0.012	
0.4mm jewellery wire	0.4	26	0.015	
Intermediate wires				
24-gauge floristry wire	0.5	24	0.020	
0.5mm coloured craft wire	0.5	24	0.020	
0.6mm jewellery wire	0.6	22	0.025	
Strong wires				
1.2mm jewellery wire	1.2	16	0.050	
Aluminium wires				
1.5mm	1.5	15	0.0571	
2mm	2	12	0.0808	Thick

★ Soft beading/binding wires

These are soft wires that are used in the creation of cake crowns and beaded garlands. They include:
☆ **0.3mm copper craft wire** – a wonderful soft wire, enamelled in a wide range of colours.
☆ **28-gauge beading wire** – with a steel core that can be quite rough on your fingers.
☆ **0.4mm jewellery wire** – slightly firmer than the above but ideal if you want a chunkier effect, not ideal for beginners.
☆ **Bullion wire** – a crinkly wire used by many crafts – I often use this to make beaded garlands.

★ Intermediate wires

These are stronger wires that can support a little weight. They are used to create cake fountains, wired cake tops and elements of cake crowns, such as coils.
☆ **Straight, paper-covered, steel floristry wire**, available in many gauges with 24-gauge being the recommended strength for cake fountains. This wire is not suitable for cake crowns.
☆ **0.5mm coloured craft wire and 0.6mm jewellery wire**, ideal for bead support on cake crowns. This wire is also thin enough to go through the holes in most beads so lends itself to beaded cake toppers. The difference between them is that the craft wire has a copper core so is softer and the jewellery wire has a steel core so is harder.

★ Strong wires

Heavy-duty wires used for the base of cake crowns.
☆ **1.2mm jewellery wire** – this is the wire that you bind all your cake crown elements to. For beginners this wire is ideal as it retains its shape, however as you become more proficient at binding you may find aluminium wire easier to use.

★ Aluminium wire

This is available in many widths but for cake decorations I would recommend **1.5mm and 2mm**. The wire is wonderful to work with as it can easily be bent to create any shape you wish; it is also available in an ever-increasing range of colours, opening up all sorts of possibilities for cake decorators.

Beads

Beads can be used to complement a cake design or be used in their own right as the principal decoration on a cake. There is a huge choice of beads available from around the world, from cheap plastic to expensive crystal – which you choose for your cake project will depend on your budget and the effect you are trying to create.

★ Sizes

Beads range in size from tiny seed beads to large beads designed to be worn as pendants. 6mm (¼in) and 8mm (⁵⁄₁₆in) beads tend to be the most frequently used in cake jewellery, although smaller beads such as silver-lined Japanese Rocailles are used to add sparkle and larger beads are added to create interesting focal points.

★ Shapes

Most people think of beads as round but of course they are available in a variety of shapes. Round beads are the most frequently used for cake jewellery but heart, star and cut-crystal shapes are often appropriate too.

★ A mix of colours

Cake jewellery is most effective when it reflects the other colours used on the cake including the icing so, for example, if a cake is covered with ivory sugarpaste then it helps to have a few ivory pearls in the jewellery to bring the design together. Blending and contrasting colour schemes also work well. I recommend using about six different shades, however this is only a guide – there is no right or wrong.

★ Selecting beads

It is a good idea to place the beads you have chosen for a project together on a bead mat so you can see what they look like together. This also enables you to add or subtract beads to achieve a pleasing balance between the colours and shapes.

Garlands

If you have never made any cake jewellery before, garlands are a good place to start, as they are very straightforward to create and look really attractive around the base of a cake.

1 Choose your selection of beads – you'll need a range of sizes and colours and some soft beading wire either 0.3mm craft wire, bullion wire or similar in a suitable colour. Thread a selection of beads onto the wire but do not cut the wire from the reel at this stage.

2 Hold the last bead threaded on in one hand and the wire, either side of the bead, in the other hand and twist the bead onto the wire. Keep twisting until the end of the wire is twisted in.

3 Leave a space and rotate the next bead one and a half times around to secure it in place. Repeat for the remaining beads on the wire. You can vary the spaces between the beads, to prevent them bunching when they are placed around your cake. A good rule of thumb is that the smaller the beads, the closer together you should twist them.

4 Once you have twisted all the beads onto the wire, cut the wire and twist the end into the garland. Check that the garland is long enough to go around the base of the cake a few times. If the garland looks a bit sparse, make another garland smaller than the first. Arrange the garland loosely around the base of the cake, interweaving the ends so that they are secure.

Tip

Usually a garland should go around a cake three times. However this depends on the beads you have used so experiment to see what you prefer.

All Dressed Up
A simple strung garland around the base of this mini-cake lifts the design into a new dimension.

Simple Fountains

A jewellery fountain adds a wonderful touch of glamour and glitz to a cake, perfect for a special occasion. They are not difficult to create – you need beads, 24-gauge floristry wire and a little jewellery glue. Fountains are best created in two stages to allow the glue time to dry.

Fabulous Fountain
A beaded fountain adds a sensational finish to this lovely floral tiered cake.

1 Select beads to match or complement your cake. Squeeze out a little jewellery glue onto your work surface. Dip the end of the wire into the glue, place a bead on top of the glue and leave to dry horizontally.

2 Use a cocktail stick (toothpick) to place a dot of glue on the wire for the bead furthest from the end. Thread the bead on so that it rests on the glue dot. Repeat along the wire until the desired effect is created. Experiment with different bead combinations, making between three and six of each of your chosen types, plus one for the centre. I recommend using about 25 wires in total.

Tip
The more beads used the less wires you will need – when it comes to arranging them, it is a lot easier to use a pair of pliers than your fingers.

3 Find the centre of the top tier by folding a paper circle the same size as the cake in half and half again and placing it on the top of the cake. Mark the centre, where the folds cross, with a pin. Insert a posy pick vertically into the centre of the cake so that its surface is fractionally below the surface of the sugarpaste – wires must not be pushed directly into cake. Add a small amount of oasis fix to secure the wires.

4 Gently curve the wires by wrapping them around a cylinder. Cut the wires to an appropriate length for your cake and insert into the posy pick.

5 Create the basic shape of the topper by firstly arranging some curved wires of the same length around the base of the fountain and then add the straight central wire to define the height. Fill in the spaces with the remaining wires, making sure that they are evenly spaced.

Aluminium Shapes

Stunning cake decorations can be made very easily by bending coloured aluminium wire to shape. Simply insert a posy pick into your cake and arrange the shapes you have created – what could be more striking? Here are a few simple ideas, however this wire is so easy to bend and use that I am sure you will be experimenting with your own ideas in no time!

Making a coil

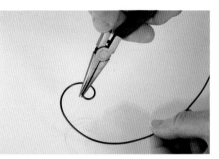

Cut lengths of aluminium wire, hold the centre of the wire using your fingers or some jewellery pliers and bend the wire into a loose coil. Experiment to see how loose or tight you prefer the coil.

Simple coiled heart

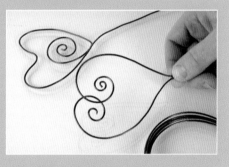

Coil the ends of two lengths of wire then twist these together so they create a heart shape. Insert the ends into a posy pick.

Dragonfly Dreams
Wire coils provide the focal point of this unusual cake design, and echo the insect motif on the side.

Bending to a template

Using a template enables you to repeat shapes easily and helps you keep outlines symmetrical. Draw a template onto card. When experimenting with your own shapes, keep it simple and draw a continuous line.

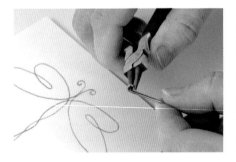

1 To create a perfect, tight circle at the end of your chosen wire, clasp one end of the wire between round-nose pliers and wrap the wire around one side of the pliers.

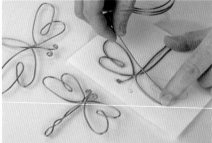

2 Place the wire over the template. Press down on the circle with the finger of one hand while bending the wire to shape following the lines of the template with your other hand. Reposition the finger that is pressing down on the wire as necessary.

Crowns

Adding a jewellery crown to the top or base of a cake can easily turn a very simply decorated cake into a stunning centrepiece. Crowns can be made well in advance of an occasion and popped on at the last moment. There are many ways to decorate a crown – the next few pages give you a range of ideas for different elements to get you started and then show you how to assemble everything together.

Diving for Pearls
This sparkling cake features a crown of twisted pearl elements around the base, which sets the design apart.

Simple twisted elements

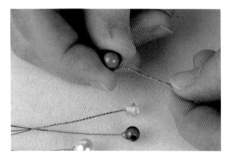

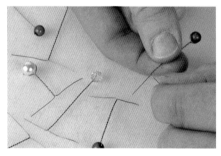

1 Take a bead and thread it onto a cut length of 0.3mm coloured craft wire. Using the thumb and index finger of one hand, hold the bead in the middle of the wire then bring the wires together between your thumb and index finger of your other hand to lock the bead in position.

2 Twist the bead repeatedly while slowly allowing the wire in your other hand to slide through your fingers to obtain an even twist.

3 Twist the wire to an appropriate length then separate the wires to form a 'T' shape. Repeat as necessary.

Multiple beads on a twisted wire

Tip
The secret of an even twist is releasing the wire with even pressure.

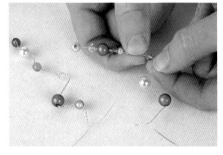

1 Twist a bead on a 0.3mm wire as described above. Stop the twist about 1cm (⅜in) from the end. Thread more beads onto the twisted wire then separate the wires to form a 'T' shape.

2 Shape the twisted wire to create a zigzag – the bends of the zigzag hold the beads at different heights. Repeat as required.

Group of beads on a stem

Thread a selection of beads onto a length of 0.3mm wire. Bring the beads to the centre of the wire then using your thumb and the index finger of one hand, hold the beads in place while you bring the wires together with your thumb and the index finger of your other hand so that the beads are locked into position. Twist the beads repeatedly while slowly allowing the wire in your other hand to slide through your fingers to obtain an even twist. Repeat as required.

Pink Paradise
The beads used in the crown around the base of this mini-cake and the statement beads in the topper match the colours of the paste perfectly,

Statement beads

These can be used as crown elements or inserted into a posy pick as an alternative top decoration.

1 Cut lengths of 0.5mm coloured craft wire. Take a length and clasp one end of the wire between round-nose pliers and wrap the wire around one side of the pliers to create a perfect circle in the wire.

2 Place a dab of jewellery glue on the wire next to the circle and thread on a bead so that it rests on the glue. Allow to dry in a suitable position, repeat as required. Once the glue has dried, measure 2.5cm (1in) from the end of each wire and bend the wire to create an 'L' shape.

Fixing beads with crimps

Crimps are tiny metal beads that are crushed to hold beads in place on a wire. Use this technique to create crown elements or freeform cake-top decorations.

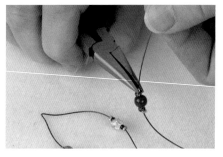

1 Thread a crimp followed by a bead or beads and another crimp onto 0.5mm coloured craft wire. Using a pair of flat-nose pliers or crimping pliers, squash the first crimp to secure it.

2 Pick up the wire and allow the beads and loose crimp to slip down the wire to sit snugly next to the squashed crimp. Squash the second crimp to secure all the beads in place.

Abstract Reasons
Wire can be bent into abstract shapes as well as regular coils, and crimps enable you to position beads wherever you like, as on this topper.

Wire coils

Interesting crown elements can also be created from wire alone. Here is one example that I think works particularly well.

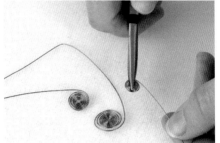

1 Cut approximately 25cm (10in) of 0.5mm coloured craft wire, clasp one end of the wire between round-nose pliers and wrap the wire around one side of the pliers to create a perfect circle in the wire.

2 Hold the circle horizontally in a pair of flat-nose pliers and with your spare hand push the wire away from you so it wraps around the circle. Reposition the circle and wrap around about a quarter of the circle, before repositioning again. When it is large enough to hold in your fingers, continue coiling by hand until it is the desired size. Bend the end to create an 'L' shape to attach to the crown.

Assembling crowns

To assemble all the elements of your crown, you need some 0.3mm coloured craft wire for binding and a base wire on which to bind. Choose either strong jewellery wire (ideal for beginners as it retains its shape) or aluminium wire (easier if you are more proficient at binding).

Crowning Glory
The crown on the cake shown at the start of this chapter was assembled using the steps here.

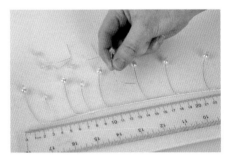
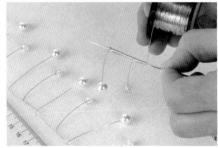
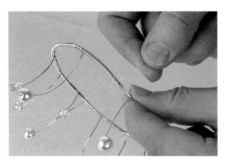

1 Decide on the circumference of your crown and cut a length of base wire to this length or slightly larger. A cake board is useful to measure the wire. Straighten the wire and plan the placement of your elements, ensuring that repeat patterns are evenly spaced. Planning crowns also gives you a good indication as to whether you have created enough elements.

2 Starting near one end, hold one of the prepared wire 'T' or 'L' shapes onto the base wire and wrap the 0.3mm wire around both wires on one side of the 'T' to bind the two together neatly. Hold the next 'T' in position and continue binding tightly along the wire.

3 Continue this process adding the 'T' shapes every few centimetres. To join the crown together, continue binding until you reach the end of the wire then abut or fractionally overlap the two ends of the base wire and continue binding the 'T's until you reach your start point.

Tip

If your binding is not a neat as you would like, wrap a small garland of beads around the base wire to add interest and hide any imperfections.

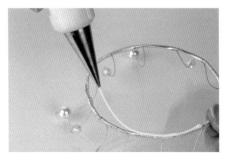

4 If necessary, adjust the shape of the base of the crown to create a circle. Using a cake board is very helpful when reshaping a crown. To attach the crown to the cake, use royal icing coloured to match your cake and pipe icing along the underside of the crown. Place the crown centrally on top of the top tier. Take a damp paintbrush and neaten any visible royal icing, if necessary. Allow to dry.

Projects

★ Modern Masterpiece
Carving chapter, page 33

You will need:

☆ 7.5cm (3in) deep round cakes: 25.5cm (10in), 18cm (7in), 10cm (4in)
☆ 30.5cm (12in) round cake drum
☆ Round hardboard cake boards: 18cm (7in), 12.5cm (5in), 6.5cm (2½in)
☆ Sugarpaste: 3kg (6½lb) white
☆ Modelling paste: 100g (3½oz) red, 75g (3oz) pink, 60g (2oz) black, 50g (2oz) each purple, yellow, green, light blue, white, 25g (1oz) navy
☆ Stay-fresh mats or clear plastic bags
☆ Selection of round cutters including piping tubes (tips) PME no. 16, 17, 18
☆ Craft knife
☆ Straight edge and set square
☆ Multi-sized ribbon cutter (FMM)
☆ Royal icing
☆ Sugar glue
☆ 15mm (½in) wide black ribbon

Instructions:

1 Carve the cakes following the guidance on pages 36–37.

2 Place each cake on the appropriate hardboard cake board and place on waxed paper. Separately cover the cakes and cake drum with the white sugarpaste. Allow to dry.

3 Dowel the two lower tiers and stack the cakes on the covered board, securing in place with royal icing.

5 Roll out each of the modelling pastes between narrow spacers and cover with stay-fresh mats or clear plastic to prevent the pastes drying out.

6 Cut out a selection of straight-sided shapes, using a straight edge and a craft knife. Starting at the base of each tier, attach the shapes in position on the cake using sugar glue. Adjust the size, fit and angle of the shapes as required once on the cake using the craft knife and straight edge. You may find it useful to refer to the steps on page 73 as many of the shapes need to fit snugly next to one another.

7 Create concentric circles using the circle cutters, as shown on page 74, and attach whole or partial circles as desired onto the cake.

8 Add further inlay pieces, referring to my cake or Kandinsky's paintings for inspiration.

9 Cut some thin black modelling paste strips using the multi-sized ribbon cutter. Allow to dry fractionally then position on the cake, using a set square to ensure perfect straightness. Trim to size with a craft knife.

★ Patchwork Heart
Colour chapter, page 39

You will need:

☆ 20cm (8in) round cake
☆ 30.5cm (12in) round cake drum
☆ Sugarpaste: red, black, cream, brown, white
☆ Modelling paste: pink, black, white, mixture of creams and browns, red

☆ Stencils: peony cake top design (LC), leafy scroll top design (DS – C357)
☆ Craft knife
☆ Dresden tool
☆ Silhouette template (see page 157)
☆ Lace
☆ Black edible paste colour
☆ Paper towel
☆ Cutters: platform stiletto shoe cutter (LC), set of circle cutters (FMM geometric set), piping tubes (tips) PME no. 4, 16, 18
☆ Moulds: classic chrysanthemum (FI – FL271), flower set mini misc (FI – FL107)
☆ 15mm (½in) wide cream ribbon

Instructions:

1 Cover the cake drum with cream sugarpaste and emboss with the leafy scroll stencil.

2 Carve the cake as shown on page 34.

3 Cover the cake in sections. Using sugarpaste, create red and black millefiori (see page 45), arranging the sausages of paste to give an animal print effect, and add to the cake as shown.

4 Lightly marble some cream and brown sugarpaste (see page 42), roll out and emboss with the peony cake top stencil. Cut out a circle of this paste and add to the cake between the red-and-black animal print sections.

5 Emboss some white sugarpaste with lace and attach to the top of the heart.

6 Marble some more cream and brown sugarpaste colours together and use to cover the top right-hand section of the heart. Using the Dresden tool, texture the paste to represent fabric.

7 Cover the remaining area white. Then create some black-and-white dotted sugarpaste as shown on page 43 and use to make a picture frame.

8 Paint over the lace with black edible paste colour and once dry, use a paper towel to reveal the pattern, as shown on page 50.

9 Add the decoration. Make moulded flowers (see pages 115–116), then cut and add the silhouette using a craft knife and the template on page 157. Add thin strips of black-and-white stripes (see page 44). Add buttons made from marbled modelling paste and a pink shoe cut from millefiori patterned paste (see pages 42 and 45). Finally add ruffles made by folding thinly rolled-out marbled modelling paste.

Key Techniques Covering Cakes (page 26); Covering Boards (page 28); Stacking Cakes (page 30); Embossing with Stencils (page 67);

★ Perfect Poppies

Painting chapter, page 47

You will need:

☆ 12.5cm (5in) round cake
☆ 13cm (9in) round cake drum
☆ Sugarpaste: 500g (1lb 2oz) each white, red
☆ Modelling paste: black, green
☆ Flower paste: 25g (1oz) red, plus a little black and green
☆ Edible paste colours: red, black
☆ Black edible ink pen
☆ Cutters: large poppy cutter (LC), swirls (PC)
☆ Poppy petal veiner (GI)
☆ Sugar shaper
☆ Piping tube (tip): PME no. 1
☆ Royal icing: black, white
☆ Piping (pastry) bags
☆ Paintbrush and natural sponge
☆ Flower former
☆ Paper towel
☆ Ball tool and foam pad
☆ Cutting wheel (PME) and tweezers
☆ 15mm (½in) wide black ribbon

Instructions:

1 Make the poppy following the instructions on page 81.

2 Cover the cake with white sugarpaste and the cake drum with red sugarpaste and allow to dry.

3 Dilute red edible paste colour and paint five crescent-moon shapes around the side of the cake to create the base of each poppy. Immediately take a damp natural sponge and use to blot the colour into the centre of each flower. See page 49 for further guidance.

4 Once dry, draw the poppy petals and stamens with a black edible ink pen, as shown on page 51.

5 Add definition to the lower edge of each poppy by adding a thin sausage of black modelling paste made with the sugar shaper fitted with a no. 1 piping tube (tip).

6 Add a green stem to each poppy using the sugar shaper fitted with a small round disc. Pipe black royal icing dots on top of each stamen.

7 Place the cake on the cake drum, add black modelling paste trim to the join using the sugar shaper, as before.

8 Cut out six large swirls and one small swirl from black modelling paste. Allow to firm slightly then attach one large and the small swirl to the top of the cake. Trim the remaining swirls so they fit neatly around the base of the cake and attach in place.

9 Pipe white royal icing dots around the outside of each swirl.

★ Stacked Hatboxes

Stencilling chapter, page 57

You will need:

For the cakes:
☆ Round cakes: 25.5cm (10in), 20cm (8in), 15cm (6in)
☆ Round hardboard cake boards: 25.5cm (10in), 20cm (8in), 15cm (6in)
☆ 35cm (14in) round cake drum
☆ Sugarpaste: 1.6kg (3½lb) each very pale pink (board, top tier), purple (bottom tier); 500g (1lb 2oz) each pale pink (middle tier), claret (middle tier)
☆ Modelling paste: 225g (8oz) pale pink, 175g (6oz) very pale pink, 50g (2oz) each purple, claret
☆ Edible dust colours: pink (rose SK), claret (cyclamen SK), purple (violet SK), pastel pink and superwhite (SF)
☆ Royal icing
☆ Stencils: damask cake side design (DS), leafy scroll side design (DS), chic rose side design (DS), chic rose circle design (DS)
☆ Stencil side fixing kit
☆ Multi-sized ribbon cutter (FMM)
☆ Sugar shaper
☆ 15mm (½in) wide claret ribbon

For the peonies:
☆ Flower paste: 150g (5¼oz) claret, 25g (1oz) green
☆ Edible dust colours: pink (rose SK), purple (violet SK), green
☆ Large blossom cutter (OP – F6C)
☆ Random veining tool (HP)
☆ Ball tool and foam pad
☆ Peony leaf veiner (GI)
☆ Flower formers

Instructions:

1 Cover the cake drum with 800g (1¾lb) pale pink sugarpaste; emboss using the rose circle design and a smoother. Trim to fit.

2 Place each cake on the appropriate hardboard cake board and cover in two sections as shown on page 27, covering the sides before the top. This ensures a sharp edge to the top of the cake and that the join is later covered by the rim of the lid.

3 For the bottom tier: Either raise the cake up or turn the cake upside down and position the stencil so that the pattern starts at the base of the cake, using a side fixing kit. Stencil the side design using royal icing whitened with superwhite dust and tinted with claret dust colour. Repeat and mask as necessary (see page 65).

4 For the middle tier: Using narrow spacers, roll out the pale pink modelling paste into a long strip large enough to fit around the cake. Stencil the strip using the leafy scroll stencil and edible dusts (see page 60). Cut one long edge straight. Paint sugar glue over the side of the cake and carefully, with the help of an extra pair of hands if possible, transfer your stencilled paste to the cake.

5 For the top tier: Use a modelling paste strip as for the middle tier but use royal icing to stencil the design (see page 64).

6 Add appropriately coloured lid rims to all the hatboxes by rolling sugarpaste into long sausages and then rolling the paste out to an even 5mm (³⁄₁₆in) thickness. Cut strips using a multi-sized ribbon cutter and attach.

7 Neaten the top edge of each cake using modelling paste and a sugar shaper fitted with the medium ribbon disc. Add modelling paste ribbons, cut with a multi-sized ribbon cutter, as desired.

8 Dowel and stack the cakes and place on the board, leaving room for the peony.

9 Make two peonies and four sets of leaves as shown on pages 82–83 and position on the cake and board to complete.

★ Pretty in Pink
Stencilling chapter, page 63

You will need:
- ☆ 12.5cm (5in) round cake
- ☆ 20cm (8in) round cake drum
- ☆ Sugarpaste: 500g (1lb 2oz) each pink, very pale pink
- ☆ Pink sugar peony (see pages 82–83)
- ☆ Royal icing
- ☆ Pink edible paste colour
- ☆ Stencils: peony cake top design (LC), peony cake side design (LC)
- ☆ Stencil side fixing kit
- ☆ 15mm (½in) wide dusky pink ribbon

Instructions:
Separately cover the cake and cake drum with the very pale pink and pink sugarpaste. Stencil the designs onto the top and sides of the cake with the royal icing, coloured with the pink edible paste colour, as shown on pages 63–64. Place the sugar peony on the top of the cake to complete.

★ Flower Power
Cutters chapter, page 69

You will need:
- ☆ Round cakes: 20cm (8in), 15cm (6in), 10cm (4in)

- ☆ 30.5cm (12in) round cake drum
- ☆ Round hardboard cake boards: 20cm (8in), 15cm (6in), 10cm (4in)
- ☆ Sugarpaste: 1.5kg (3lb) white, 1kg (2¼lb) pink
- ☆ Modelling paste: 200g (7oz) pink, 150g (5oz) light blue, 125g (4½oz) yellow, 75g (3oz) lime green, 25g (1oz) each dark blue, white, red, 15g (½oz) dark green
- ☆ Cutters: round pastry cutters, elegant hearts (LC), flat florals set 1 (LC), large flat floral (LC), scroll and petal set (LC), daisy centre stamp (JEM), fantasy flower (PC), daisy marguerites (PME)
- ☆ Stencils: Japanese flower and scroll pattern sheet (LC), Chinese floral circle (LC)
- ☆ Royal icing
- ☆ Piping tubes (tips): PME no. 2, 4, 16, 17, 18
- ☆ Piping (pastry) bag
- ☆ Sugar shaper
- ☆ 15mm (½in) wide bright pink ribbon

Instructions:
1 Place the cakes on the appropriate sized hardboard cake boards then separately cover all the cakes with white sugarpaste.

2 Cover the cake drum with pink sugarpaste. Leave to dry.

3 Dowel and stack the cakes on the covered cake board.

4 Add a 4cm (1½in) wide pink modelling paste band to the base of the cake on the bottom tier.

5 Emboss some thinly rolled-out blue modelling paste with the Japanese flower and scroll stencil. Cut out large circles using the round pastry cutters, cut across the circles and attach in place abutting the pink strip and each other.

6 Roll out a 7.5cm (3in) wide strip of lime green modelling paste between narrow spacers. Using the pastry cutters, remove parts of circles from one long edge so that the strip can be easily abutted to the blue circles. The strip might stretch slightly as you lift it. Once in position on the cake, take some smaller circle cutters and remove part-circles from the uppermost edge so that the lime green band covers the join between the bottom two tiers and starts to go up the side of the middle tier.

7 Use a sugar shaper fitted with a small round disc to add red modelling paste trim to the top of the blue circles.

8 Create eight flowers on the base tier using the petal from the scroll and petal set, the large flat floral cutter set and daisy centre

stamp, using the techniques shown on page 72. Attach the elements of the layered flowers directly to the cake, varying the heights and positions of the petals.

9 For the middle tier, create five larger flowers and five smaller flowers using elegant hearts for the outer petals, fantasy flowers for the inner petals together with a flat floral and daisy centre stamp for the larger flowers. Emboss the light blue paste with the Chinese floral circle stencil. Attach the elements of the layered flowers directly to the cake, varying the heights and positions of the petals.

10 Add strings of yellow daisy marguerites to the board, having removed their centres with a no. 16 piping tube (tip).

11 Pipe small dots around the edge of the board using a no. 2 tube (tip) and white royal icing.

12 Add dark green rings of circles to the lime green band, using no. 17 and no. 4 piping tubes (tips) as cutters.

13 Finally, add blue daisy marguerites of different sizes to the middle and top tiers, removing the centres with piping tubes (tips). Trim and abut the shapes as required.

★ Fuchsia Fashionista
Flowers chapter, page 77

You will need:
- ☆ 25.5cm (10in) square cake
- ☆ 25.5cm (10in) square cake drum
- ☆ Templates (see pages 156–157)
- ☆ Sugarpaste: 600g (1lb 5oz) black, 1kg (2¼lb) deep pink
- ☆ Modelling paste: 300g (11oz) deep pink
- ☆ Pastillage: 50g (2oz) grey
- ☆ Sugar glue
- ☆ Edible silver lustre dust (SK)
- ☆ Confectioners' glaze
- ☆ Stencil: crewel ring top design – large 32.5cm (13in) (DS – W086CL)

Key Techniques Covering Cakes (page 26); Covering Boards (page 28); Stacking Cakes (page 30); Embossing with Stencils (page 67);

☆ Quilting tool (PME)
☆ Cutters: medium oval cutters set 2 (LC), circle cutters (FMM geometric set)
☆ Sugar shaper
☆ Dresden tool
☆ Craft knife
☆ Cutting wheel (PME)
☆ 15mm (½in) wide black-and-white ribbon

Instructions:

1 Cover the cake drum with black sugarpaste and add the stencilled pattern using the edible lustre dust, as shown on page 59. Re-trim the board and set aside to dry.

2 Make four pastillage rings using the sugar shaper fitted with the medium round disc and 2.5cm (1in) circle cutter to act as a former. Also make two 2.5cm (1in) round discs for the clasp embossing the top of each using the stencil. Once completely dry, paint with edible silver lustre dust mixed with confectioners' glaze.

3 Carve the cake using the templates, following the steps on page 35. Place the carved cake on waxed paper and cover in four sections: start by spreading a thin layer of buttercream cover the back of the bag.

4 Roll out enough sugarpaste to an even 5mm (³⁄₁₆in) thickness, ideally using spacers, to fit this area roughly. Cut one long edge of the paste straight. Pick up the paste and place on the buttercreamed section so that the cut edge is flush with the lower edge of the cake. Smooth the paste with a smoother to give an even surface.

5 Roughly cut away the excess paste with a pair of scissors – note you are just removing the excess not trying to give a neat finish. Take a cutting wheel and run it through the sugarpaste to define the side edges of the bag, both sides need to be more or less symmetrical. Then using a craft knife, cut away the excess paste. Cut the paste at the top along the central line.

6 Referring to the front template, add small sausages of sugarpaste to the front of the bag, this will help to give the appearance of pleats. Cover the front of the bag with sugarpaste, cutting to size as for the back. Using your finger and a Dresden tool to shape the sugarpaste over the sausages of paste to look like pleats.

7 Cover both ends of the bag, again cutting one end of the sugarpaste straight before adding the paste to the bag. Trim the paste

so it abuts the sugarpaste of the sides.

8 Use a Dresden tool to blend the joins between the sides and ends of the bag and to create an indention in which the seam trim will sit.

9 Using a sugar shaper, add trim to all the seams using the medium round disc, and to the clasp using the large round disc.

10 Using the template, cut the two curved pieces from thinly rolled modelling paste and attach to the front and back of the bag. Run the quilting tool around each one to create the effect of stitching.

11 Make a selection of fabric flowers from modelling paste, following the steps on pages 78–79. Attach to the front of the bag.

12 Attach the pastillage rings to the top of the bag by looping 2cm (¾in) wide strips of modelling paste through each one and attaching to the top of the curved pieces.

13 Roll two sausages of sugarpaste, 1cm (³⁄₈in) wide by 25cm (10in) long, for the handles. Thinly roll out the remaining modelling paste into a long strip, cut in half lengthways. Wrap each sausage in a strip of modelling paste, so that the modelling paste extends beyond the sausage by approximately 2cm (¾in). Thread these sections of paste through the rings on the bag and fold the paste back on itself to attach the handles. Glue the handles in place, supporting them if necessary while the glue dries.

14 Add small balls of paste to the back of the clasp discs and attach to the top of the bag using sugar glue.

15 Finally, transfer the decorated cake to the prepared board.

★ Cushion Stack

Embossing chapter, page 85

You will need:

☆ 7.5cm (3in) deep square cakes: 28cm (11in), 23cm (9in), 18cm (7in)
☆ 35.5cm (14in) square cake drum
☆ Square hardboard cake boards: 15cm (6in), 10cm (4in), 7.5cm (3in)
☆ Sugarpaste: 1.5kg ivory (3lb), 1.2kg (2lb 10oz) golden brown, 1kg (2¼lb) each navy, cream, 500g (1lb 2oz) each blue, sea green
☆ Modelling paste: lime green, aqua, navy, golden brown, white, sea green
☆ Sugar shaper
☆ Textured rolling pins: watermark taffeta (PC), orchid (PC), linen (PC)
☆ Embossers: swirls and hearts (PC), embroidery set (PC), flower embossing stamps (FMM flower 1), vine and berry embossing sticks (HP set 11), flower embroidery embossing sticks (HP set 10), small floral embossing stick (HP set 1)
☆ Cutters: paisley (LC), flat floral set 1 (LC), 55mm (2in) gerbera (PME), curled leaf (LC), stylized leaves (LC), teardrop (LC) daisy marguerites (PME), circle cutters, macro flowers (LC)
☆ Piping tubes (tips): round – PME no. 1, 2, 4, 16, 17, 18; ribbon – PME no. 32R
☆ Stencils: leafy scroll side design (DS – C358), Japanese flower and scroll pattern sheet (LC), Chinese floral circle (LC), peony cake top design (LC)
☆ Daisy mould set (FI – FL288)
☆ Dresden tool
☆ Edible paste colours: golden brown (autumn leaf – SF) lime green, blue
☆ Edible gold lustre dust (SK)
☆ Clear alcohol (such as gin or vodka)
☆ Sugar glue
☆ Cocktail sticks (toothpicks)
☆ Royal icing
☆ 15mm (½in) wide cream/ivory ribbon

Instructions:

1 Cover the board with the golden brown sugarpaste and emboss using a stencil. Once dry, sponge paint edible gold lustre dust mixed with water over the board to help highlight the pattern (see page 49).

2 Make templates: cut out squares of paper the same sizes as your cakes. Fold each in half and in half again to produce smaller squares and then fold each diagonally from the centre to the outer corner. Draw a smooth curve 3.5cm (1½in), 2.5cm (1in) or 1.5cm (½in), depending on the tier, in from the shorter side to the corner, cut along the curve then open out the templates.

3 Level the cakes. Place the templates on top and cut vertically down through each cake to create the basic shapes, as shown for the heart cake on page 34.

Layering (page 72); Abutting (page 73); Dresden Tool (page 94); Sugar Shaper (pages 96–98); Piping Dots (page 109)

4 Mark a horizontal line midway around each cake using cocktail sticks (toothpicks). Then create the rounded shape of the top of the cushions by carving from the top of the cushion to this midway line. Turn the cakes over and shape the underside of the cushions in the same way.

5 Covering one cake at a time, place a cake on waxed paper. Spread a thin layer of buttercream over the uppermost half of the cushion to fill any holes and help the sugarpaste stick. Attach the appropriate hardboard cake board to the top of the cake (this will become the base of the cake). Roll out the sugarpaste, texture the paste with a rolling pin (see page 88) and cover the top of the cushion. Trim the paste to the midway line. Turn the cake over and cover the second half in the same way. Carefully trim to size then rub the edges with your finger to make a reasonably neat seam. Smooth the cake as necessary.

6 Take the Dresden tool and indent lines coming away from either side of the seam. Soften each line by rubbing a finger over the indented paste. Vary the angle, position and length of line to give the cushions a lifelike appearance. Finally indent the seam all round the cake.

7 Decorate the cakes with modelling paste as desired. The large cushion uses many techniques from the Embossing chapter (see pages 84–91). The middle cushion uses simple cut outs (see page 71) and a sugar shaper.

8 Add trim to the seam of each cushion using modelling paste squeezed out of a sugar shaper.

9 Once the decoration is complete, highlight some of the textured panels using diluted edible paste colours and clear alcohol (see page 51). Allow to dry.

10 Dowel and stack the cakes, using royal icing to secure the tiers.

★ Gaudi's Grandeur
Tools chapter, page 93

You will need:
☆ 7.5cm (3in) deep round cakes: 20cm (8in), 12.5cm (5in)
☆ 28cm (11in) round cake drum
☆ Round hardboard cake boards: 12.5cm (5in), 9cm (3.5in)
☆ Sugarpaste: 2.2kg (4¾lb) ivory
☆ Modelling paste: teal, light aqua, pink, orange, ivory, purple
☆ Scriber
☆ Eight-point star templates (see page 155)
☆ Carnation cutter set (FMM)
☆ Piping tubes (tips): PME no. 16, 18
☆ Sugar shaper
☆ Craft knife
☆ Cutting wheel (PME)
☆ Straight edge
☆ Sugar glue
☆ Cocktail sticks (toothpicks)
☆ Edible ink pen (any colour)
☆ Royal icing
☆ 15mm (½in) wide teal ribbon

Instructions:
1 Carve the cakes following the step-by-step instructions on pages 36–37.

2 Place each cake on the appropriate hardboard cake board and place on waxed paper. Separately cover both cakes and the cake drum with the sugarpaste. Allow to dry.

3 Dowel the larger cake and stack the cakes on the covered board, but do not stick them at this stage.

4 Take a scriber and scribe around the base of each tier. Unstack the cakes, you should now have a scribed circle on the covered board and the top of the larger cake.

5 Check the star templates fit snugly up against your scribed circles and adjust their shape if necessary. Roll out the light aqua

modelling paste between narrow spacers and cut the three stars using the templates and a craft knife. Place in position on the cake, and then add a little sugar glue just to the points of the stars.

6 Create the inlay flowers using the carnation cutters (see page 74). Add embossed lines to the pattern using a cutting wheel.

7 Remove circles from the design using piping tubes (tips) and replace with small balls of paste. Flatten each ball slightly to give a domed appearance.

8 Stack the cakes inside the scribed circles, ensuring that the star decorations abut the sides of the cakes.

9 Mark the tips of the two-coloured pink and teal star points with cocktail sticks (toothpicks), using a straight edge to help line them up. Refer to the photo for guidance and note that the points are longer down the sides of the cakes than they are on the top.

10 Roll out the pink and teal paste between narrow spacers. Cut out a star from the centre of each using one of the templates, making sure there is enough paste around the star to create the points.

11 Using the straight edge, line up two opposite points of the star and cut eight radial lines across the star, continuing the line to the edge of the paste each time. Remove the central star.

12 Take a cut section and place on the cake abutting one edge with the central star and one straight edge with the cocktail stick (toothpick) marker. Take a craft knife and straight edge and cut the paste from the tip of the light aqua star to the stick, as shown on page 100. Repeat until all stars are complete.

13 Take the edible ink pen and draw the wavy edge to the design directly onto the cake (see page 51).

14 Make templates for each wavy section using waxed paper and number them to prevent them getting mixed up. Divide each template into four then use to cut out sections of thinly rolled-out modelling paste. Attach each section to the cake as it is cut.

15 Add borders and wavy lines with a sugar shaper. Complete by adding balls of pink paste at intervals along the orange borders.

Key Techniques   Covering Cakes (page 26); Covering Boards (page 28); Stacking Cakes (page 30); Embossing with Stencils (page 67);

★ Coral Creation

Piping chapter, page 103

You will need:

☆ Round cakes: 18cm (7in), 10cm (4in)
☆ Round cake drums: 28cm (11in), 20cm (8in), 12.5cm (5in)
☆ Sugarpaste: 800g (1¾lb) each dark coral, mid coral, 500g (1lb 2oz) white with a touch of coral, 400g (14oz) light coral
☆ Modelling paste: 25g (1oz) of all four sugarpaste colours
☆ Piping tubes (tips): PME no. 1, 2, 16
☆ Reusable piping (pastry) bag and coupler
☆ Royal icing
☆ Superwhite dust (SF)
☆ Sugar shaper
☆ Flower template (see page 157)
☆ 15mm (½in) wide coral ribbon

Instructions:

1 Cover the cakes and cake drums with the appropriate colours, bringing the sugarpaste over the sides of the two smaller cake drums.

2 Using the template, emboss or scribe flowers onto the cakes and largest board. Note – which method you use will determine if the sugarpaste has to be soft or crusted over (see page 53).

3 Add a little superwhite dust to the royal icing and use to brushwork embroider the flowers (see page 111).

4 Dowel the large cake and stack the cakes.

5 Thinly roll out the white modelling paste and cut out circles with the no.16 piping tube (tip) (see page 71) then arrange these randomly over the stacked cake.

6 Pipe small dots around each circle and in the centres of the flowers using a no.1 piping tube (tip).

7 Fit the medium sized round disc into the sugar shaper and add trim of the appropriate colour to the base of the two smaller drums.

8 Change to the small round disc and add curved lines to the cakes.

★ Prettiest Posy

Moulds chapter, page 113

You will need:

☆ 10cm (4in) ball cake
☆ 23cm (9in) round cake drum
☆ Sugarpaste: 1kg (2¼lb) white
☆ Modelling paste: 200g (7oz) each purple, green, white, 25g (1oz) cream
☆ Stencil: turn of the century 18cm (7in) medallion (DC – C333)
☆ Moulds: classic chrysanthemum (Fl – FL271), chrysanthemum (Fl – FL270), roses galore (Fl – FL248), medium flower set (Fl – FL306)
☆ Edible dust colours: snowflake lustre, lime green, cream, deep purple
☆ Multi-sized ribbon cutter (FMM)
☆ Sugar glue
☆ 15mm (½in) wide purple ribbon

Instructions:

1 Cover the cake drum with white sugarpaste and add the stencil design using snowflake lustre dust (see page 59). Re-trim the paste around the edge of the board.

2 Cover the cake with white sugarpaste.

3 Using the modelling pastes and the suggested moulds, make a selection of moulded flowers (see page 115). Dust the centres of some of the flowers with appropriate edible dust colours.

4 Using sugar glue, attach the moulded flowers to the ball cake, overlapping their petals so that they look natural.

5 Transfer the ball to the centre of the prepared board.

6 Thinly roll out the cream modelling paste and cut ribbons using the multi-sized ribbon cutter. Attach one long ribbon to the top of the ball, twist it a couple of times and drape it over the ball and around the board. Make two loops and attach to the top of the ball, finally add a centre to the bow.

★ Crowning Glory

Cake Jewellery chapter, page 123

You will need:

☆ 12.5cm (5in) round cake
☆ 20cm (8in) round cake drum
☆ Sugarpaste: 425g (15oz) pale dusky pink, 350g (12½oz) lilac
☆ Modelling paste: 50g (1¾oz) each plum, deep pink, dusky purple
☆ Royal icing
☆ Edible dust colours: superwhite (SF), a touch of dusky pink, autumn leaf (SF)
☆ Piping tube (tip): PME no. 1
☆ Piping (pastry) bag
☆ 3.5cm (1½in) circle cutter (FMM geometric set)
☆ Set square
☆ 15mm (½in) wide deep pink ribbon

Cake jewellery:

Wire:
☆ 1.5mm silver aluminium wire/strong jewellery wire
☆ 0.5mm and 0.3mm warm silver craft wire
☆ Rose pink bullion wire

Beads:
☆ 8mm, 6mm, 5mm, 4mm ivory pearls
☆ 6mm purple wooden beads
☆ 6mm amethyst crackle beads
☆ 4mm, 5mm, 6mm clear Swarovski crystals
☆ 6mm rose Swarovski crystals
☆ 6mm dusty pink miracle beads
☆ Purple and pink rocailles
☆ Silver crimps

Abutting (page 73); Cutting Wheel (page 89); Sugar Shaper (pages 96–98); Multi-Sized Ribbon Cutter (page 99); Piping Dots (page 109)

Cake Instructions:

1 Separately cover the cake and cake drum with sugarpaste. Once dry position the cake on the board.

2 Roll out the plum modelling paste between narrow spacers and cut out seven circles. Cut each in half and position carefully on the cake leaving a 1mm (1/32in) gap between each one.

3 Add the second and third rows using the claret and dusky pink modelling paste, following the steps on page 73. Remember to leave a 1mm (1/32in) gap between the first row of circles to give you the correct shape.

4 Make a card template of the shape for the fourth layer and use to scribe the shape onto the cake (see page 53).

5 For the fifth layer, create a slightly deeper template and also scribe this onto the cake.

6 Scribe radial lines onto the board and vertical lines between the scribed shapes using a set square.

7 Using the no. 1 piping tube (tip), pipe small dots along all the scribed lines and around the top of the first row of circles with royal icing coloured with the edible dusts.

Jewellery instructions:

1 Create seven statement beads using 8mm pearls and the 0.5mm wire (see page 130).

2 Create seven groups of beads using 0.3mm wire (see page 130).

3 Wire these elements onto aluminium or strong jewellery wire, following the instructions on page 131. Bring the ends together and create a crown.

4 Create small lengths of beaded garlands using a selection of small beads and bullion wire (see page 126). Tightly wrap the garlands around the base of the crown.

6 Pipe royal icing around the underside of the crown and position the crown in place on the cake (see page 131).

★ Fabulous Fountain
Cake Jewellery chapter, page 127

You will need:
☆ Round cakes: 10cm (4in), 6cm (2.5in)
☆ 18cm (7in) round cake drum
☆ Round hardboard cake boards: 10cm (4in), 6cm (2.5in)
☆ Sugarpaste: white with a touch of peach, blue
☆ Modelling paste: light orange, dark orange, blue, navy blue, white with a touch of peach
☆ Royal icing
☆ Superwhite dust (SF)
☆ Peach edible paste colour
☆ Modern flowers stencil (DS – C559)
☆ Cutters: 18mm (3/4in) daisy marguerite (PME), blossom plungers (PME), 15mm (1/2in) six-petal flower (LC flat floral set 1)
☆ Daisy centre stamp (JEM)
☆ 15mm (1/2in) wide blue ribbon

Cake jewellery:
Wire:
☆ 24g kingfisher blue jewellery wire
Beads:
☆ 6mm, 8mm orange wooden beads
☆ 6mm blue miracle beads
☆ 6mm amber miracle beads
☆ 4mm, 6mm ivory beads
☆ Turquoise crackle beads
☆ Gold rocailles
☆ Posy pick
☆ Oasis fix

Instructions:
Cover the cake board with the blue sugarpaste. Once dry, stencil flowers using royal icing coloured with superwhite dust and a touch of peach edible paste colour (see page 63). Place each cake on its

hardboard cake board and separately cover with the sugarpaste. Insert a posy pick into the centre of the smaller cake. Dowel the larger cake and once dry, stack the cakes on the prepared board using royal icing to secure the tiers. Add a selection of cut-out modelling paste flowers to the top of each cake and randomly attach a few over the board. Add flower centres using modelling paste and a daisy centre stamp. Create the fountain as shown on page 127.

★ Dragonfly Dreams
Cake Jewellery chapter, page 128

You will need:
☆ 10cm (4in) round cake
☆ 18cm (7in) round cake drum
☆ Sugarpaste: red, yellow
☆ Modelling paste: dark green, red, white, blue, navy blue
☆ Cutters: small teardrop (LC), small oval (LC), flame (LC), curled leaves (LC), 85mm (3½in), 68mm (2½in) and 55mm (2in) gerberas (PME), 18mm (3/4in) daisy marguerite (PME), 15mm (1/2in) six-petal cutter (LC flat floral set 1)
☆ Cutting wheel (PME)
☆ Cupped flower formers
☆ 1.5mm aluminium wire: royal blue, kingfisher blue
☆ Posy pick
☆ Paper towel
☆ Piping tubes (tips): PME no. 16, 17

Instructions:
Cover the cake and cake drum with sugarpaste and allow to dry. Thinly roll out the modelling pastes and cut out the required shapes. Starting with the oval of

Key Techniques Covering Cakes (page 26); Covering Boards (page 28); Covering Mini-Cakes (page 28); Stacking Cakes (page 30);

the dragonfly's body, attach the shapes to the cake. Overlap small red teardrops to create the tail and add texture to the flame shapes with a cutting wheel to create wings. Insert a posy pick into the top of the cake. Cut out three sizes of gerberas and remove a central circle from each using a no. 17 piping tube (tip). Place in cupped formers of suitable sizes, the petals should just curl over the rim of the formers. Allow the paste to dry partially, so it keeps its shape but has some movement, then place the largest flower on top of the cake lining up the circle with the top of the posy pick. Place a little twisted paper towel under the petals to help the flower retain its shape. Repeat for the remaining gerberas. Create coils of aluminium wire (see page 128) and arrange inside the posy pick.

★ Bring Out the Bunting
Colour chapter, page 44

You will need:
☆ 6cm (2½in) mini-cake
☆ Sugarpaste: white
☆ Modelling paste: green, lime green, white, dark pink, light pink
☆ Craft knife
☆ Small triangle cutter (LC)
☆ Multi-sized ribbon cutter fitted with the zigzag wheels (FMM)
☆ Sugar shaper
☆ Ball tool and foam pad
☆ Five-petal blossom cutters (PME)
☆ Piping tube (tip): PME no. 2

Instructions:
Cover the mini-cake with white sugarpaste. Create a selection of striped and checked pastes using the modelling pastes (see page 44). Cut a band of green checks and place this around the base of the cake. Cut small triangles from the patterned pastes. Thinly roll out some lime green modelling

paste and cut three zigzag strips using the multi-sized ribbon cutter. Attach these to the top of the cake as shown. Arrange the triangles to look like bunting. Add pink trim to the top of the green checks using a sugar shaper fitted with the small round disc. Add small light pink balls to the joins in the bunting. Create a dark pink cupped flower (see page 95). Using the larger edge of the piping tube (tip) cut a circle from striped modelling paste and remove two holes with the small end to create a button. Add the button to the centre of the flower.

★ Cool Blues
Painting chapter, page 48

You will need:
☆ 5cm (2in) mini-cake
☆ 10cm (4in) hardboard cake board
☆ Sugarpaste: white
☆ Modelling paste: navy, blue, light green, dark green
☆ Royal icing
☆ Piping (pastry) bag fitted with a coupler
☆ Edible paste colours: mint green, navy blue, blue
☆ Cutters: Indian scrolls (LC), paisleys (LC), small teardrop (LC), six-petal flower (LC flat floral set 1), daisy marguerites (PME)
☆ Piping tubes (tips): PME no. 1, 2
☆ Sugar shaper
☆ Dresden tool

Instructions:
Cover and flood paint the cake board as shown on page 48. Cover the cake and decorate using the modelling pastes and cutters, layering the shapes. Place the cake on the board, add green sugarpaste trim along the join and the very base of the board using a sugar shaper fitted with the small round disc. Texture as shown on page 94. Pipe dots in white royal icing to highlight the shapes.

★ London Calling
Painting chapter, page 54

You will need:
☆ 6cm (2.5in) mini-cake
☆ Sugarpaste: white
☆ Montage or picture to paint
☆ Waxed paper
☆ Edible ink pens
☆ Selection of edible paste colours
☆ Good quality paintbrushes including a 0 and 0000
☆ Clear alcohol (such as gin or vodka)

Instructions:
Create a montage of images that you wish to paint, or use my template (see page 156). Cover the mini-cake with white sugarpaste and transfer the montage to the cake using waxed paper and edible ink pens as shown on page 51. Allow the sugarpaste to dry. Dilute the paste colours in clear alcohol and paint the picture following the step-by-step instructions on page 54.

Tip
When baking mini-cakes, leave them to cool in the tin rather than trying to turn them out onto a wire rack.

Layering (page 72); Abutting (page 73); Sugar Shaper (pages 96–98); Multi-Sized Ribbon Cutter (page 99); Piping Dots (page 109)

★ Rajasthan Rose
Cutters chapter, page 72

You will need:
☆ 5cm (2in) mini-cake
☆ Sugarpaste: pale peach
☆ Modelling paste: navy blue, orange, coral
☆ Cutters: fantasy flowers (PC), flat floral sets 1 and 2 (LC), small teardrop (LC), small flame (LC), piping tube (tip) PME no. 16
☆ Ball tool and foam pad
☆ Royal icing
☆ Piping tube (tip): PME no. 1.5
☆ Piping (pastry) bag

Instructions:
Cover the mini-cake with the pale peach sugarpaste. Thinly roll out the modelling pastes and cut out a selection of shapes using the suggested cutters. Emboss the large orange flower with a fantasy flower and cup the coral one (see page 95). Then attach all the cut-out pieces to the cake, layering as desired. Finish by piping royal icing dots around the shapes.

★ Mosaic Marvel
Cutters chapter, page 75

You will need:
☆ 6cm (2.5in) mini-cake
☆ Sugarpaste: white
☆ Modelling paste: green, blue, purple, red, deep pink, pink, orange, yellow
☆ Cutters: small teardrops (LC), piping tube

(tip) PME no. 16
☆ Craft knife
☆ Cutting wheel (PME)
☆ Palette knife

Instructions:
Cover the mini-cake with white sugarpaste and allow to dry. For the decoration follow the steps on page 75.

★ Floral Elegance
Flowers chapter, page 80

You will need:
☆ 5cm (2in) mini-cake
☆ 10cm (4in) hardboard cake board
☆ Sugarpaste: coral pink, ivory with a touch of pink
☆ Modelling paste: coral pink, ivory with a touch of pink
☆ Textured wallpaper
☆ Confectioners' glaze
☆ Ball tool and foam pad
☆ Cupped former
☆ Cutters: 2.7cm (1in) wide rose petal (FMM), curled leaf set (LC), small teardrops (LC)
☆ Piping tube (tip): PME no. 3
☆ Ivory royal icing
☆ Piping (pastry) bag
☆ Narrow cream ribbon

Instructions:
Create the decorated board using wallpaper as shown on page 90. Cover the mini-cake with sugarpaste and allow to dry. Place the cake in the centre of the prepared board. Thinly roll out the ivory modelling paste and cut out shapes using the curled leaf and teardrop cutters. Attach these shapes to the cake as desired. Make a flower as shown on page 80 and attach to the top of the mini-cake using a little royal icing. Pipe royal icing dots around the lower edge of the cake and on the cake as shown.

★ Sewing Sensation
Embossing chapter, page 91

You will need:
☆ 5cm (2in) mini-cake
☆ 12.5cm (5in) hardboard cake board
☆ Sugarpaste: white, light grey
☆ Modelling paste: green
☆ Pastillage: grey
☆ Embossers: scrolls set 1 (FMM), small floral embossing stamps (HP)
☆ Glass-headed pin
☆ Sugar shaper
☆ Royal icing
☆ Edible paste colours: blue, pink, brown
☆ Piping tube (tip): PME no. 1
☆ Piping (pastry) bags
☆ Edible silver lustre dust (SK)
☆ Confectioners' glaze
☆ 12.5cm (5in) acrylic disc
☆ Design or template (see page 156)
☆ Narrow pale blue ribbon

Instructions:
Create the embossed board as shown on page 91 using white sugarpaste. Make the needle by squeezing out a short length of grey pastillage from the sugar shaper fitted with the medium round disc. Roll one end to a point, then cut the eye in the other end with a craft knife and open slightly. Allow to dry thoroughly. Carve away the top corners of the cake to create a rounded top and slightly taper the sides. Cover the cake with light grey sugarpaste and emboss rings of pattern around the base, using the different embossers. Then use the end of a glass-headed pin to emboss the remainder of the cake. Allow to dry. Mix the lustre dust with confectioners' glaze and paint the thimble and needle. Pipe coloured stitches onto the prepared board with royal icing. Create a length of thread using the sugar shaper with modelling paste and the small round disc. Feed the thread through the eye of the needle and place on the board to complete.

Key Techniques Covering Boards (page 28); Covering Mini-Cakes (page 28); Cutting Out Shapes (page 71); Ball Tool (page 95);

★ Peachy Petals

Tools chapter, page 95

You will need:

☆ 5cm (2in) mini-cake
☆ Sugarpaste: dark peach
☆ Modelling paste: dark peach, white with a hint of peach, navy
☆ Ball tool and foam pad
☆ Royal icing
☆ Piping tube (tip): PME no. 1
☆ Piping (pastry) bag
☆ Cutters: curled leaf set (LC), flat floral set 2 (LC), blossom plungers (PME), 43mm (1¾in) five-petal cutter (PME)

Instructions:

Cover the mini-cake with the sugarpaste. Create curled leaves by stroking the ball tool over curled leaf modelling paste shapes and attach to the cake. Make two cupped flowers (see page 95) and attach as shown. Add a navy centre to the flower. Add a couple of small cupped blossoms. Finally, add piped royal icing dots as desired.

★ Fuzzy Flowers

Tools chapter, page 98

You will need:

☆ 6cm (2.5in) mini-cake
☆ Sugarpaste: ivory
☆ Modelling paste: deep pink, light pink, dark green, lime green, orange, brown, ivory
☆ Cutters: carnation (FMM), piping tubes (tips) PME no. 2, 4, 18, blossom plunger cutter (PME), six-petal cutter (LC flat floral set 1)
☆ Sugar shaper
☆ Dresden tool

Instructions:

Cover the mini-cake with the sugarpaste. Thinly roll out the modelling pastes and cut out flowers and circles. Arrange on the cake, referring to the photo. Make some flower centres by rolling small balls of paste and attach to half of the flowers, flattening each slightly. Create small tufts using the sugar shaper and small mesh disc. Add the tufts with a Dresden tool around the ball centres on half of the flowers and to the centres of the remaining larger flowers.

★ Sunburst Stripes

Tools chapter, page 100

You will need:

☆ 6cm (2.5in) mini-cake
☆ Sugarpaste: white
☆ Modelling paste: purple, orange, yellow, dark brown, chestnut, light brown, beige
☆ Craft knife
☆ Straight edge
☆ Small flower mould (FI – FL107)

Instructions:

Cover the mini-cake with white sugarpaste and allow to dry. Decorate the cake with modelling paste stripes as shown on page 100. Top with a moulded two-colour modelling paste flower (see page 116).

★ Pleased as Punch

Tools chapter, page 101

You will need:

☆ 6cm (2.5in) mini-cake
☆ Sugarpaste: purple
☆ Modelling paste: cream, golden brown
☆ Moroccan mosaic craft punch range (Xcut)
☆ Sugar glue
☆ Foam pad

Instructions:

Cover the mini-cake with sugarpaste and allow to dry. Use a selection of punches to create patterned squares and intricate modelling paste shapes, as shown on page 101. Attach to the cake using a little sugar glue. For the topper, allow the squares to dry completely on a foam pad before attaching to the cake and top with a purple ball.

★ Lovely Lace

Piping chapter, page 110

You will need:

☆ 6cm (2.5in) mini-cake
☆ Sugarpaste: purple
☆ Modelling paste: white
☆ Piping tube (tip): PME no. 1
☆ Piping (pastry) bag
☆ Royal icing
☆ Cutters: curled leaf set (LC), flame set (LC), flat florals (LC), Indian scroll (LC), small teardrop (LC)
☆ Superwhite dust (SF)

Instructions:

Cover the mini-cake with purple sugarpaste and allow to dry. Cut out shapes from thinly rolled-out white modelling paste and attach to the cake as desired, leaving enough space to add the piped details. Pipe the lace threads as shown on page 110 and finish by piping royal icing dots.

★ Falling Leaves
Moulds chapter, page 118

★ She Sells Seashells...
Moulds chapter, page 120

★ All Dressed Up
Cake Jewellery chapter, page 126

You will need:

☆ 5cm (2in) mini-cake
☆ Sugarpaste: ivory
☆ Modelling paste or flower paste: golden brown
☆ Pastillage: golden brown
☆ Cutters: maple leaf (OP), strawberry leaf (JEM), rose leaf (FMM), oak leaf (LC)
☆ Leaf veiners: maple leaf (GI), briar rose leaf (GI), lamium (dead nettle) leaf (GI), strawberry leaf (GI)
☆ Ball tool and foam pad
☆ Formers or paper towel
☆ Selection of edible dust colours in autumnal shades
☆ Sugar shaper
☆ Antique gold edible lustre dust (SK)
☆ Confectioners' glaze

Instructions:

Cover the mini-cake with the ivory sugarpaste and create pastillage swirls using a sugar shaper and the small round disc. Once dry paint the swirls with lustre dust mixed with confectioners' glaze. Insert two swirls into the top of the cake and attach one to the side, as shown. Create and colour a selection of autumn leaves, as shown on page 118. Arrange these on the cake while partially dry around the pastillage swirls.

You will need:

☆ 6cm (2.5in) mini-cake
☆ 12.5cm (5in) hardboard cake board
☆ Sugarpaste: white
☆ Modelling paste: white, black
☆ Selection of shells
☆ Moulding gel
☆ Edible paste colours: selection of shell shades
☆ Superwhite dust (SF)
☆ Soft brown sugar
☆ Sugar glue
☆ Marine and sea life tappits (FMM)
☆ Cutting wheel (PME)
☆ Narrow gold ribbon

Instructions:

Make a selection of moulded sugar seashells as shown on page 120. Separately cover the mini-cake and the cake board with the white sugarpaste. Offset the cake on the board and sprinkle soft brown sugar over the board and the top of the cake. Arrange the sugar shells on the board and cake, using sugar glue to secure. Cut seaweed from thinly rolled-out black modelling paste with a cutting wheel, and cut a small anchor using the FMM cutter. Attach as desired.

Tip
If your shell mould is not successful on the first attempt, re-melt the gel and have another try.

You will need:

☆ 5cm (2.5in) mini-cake
☆ Sugarpaste: white with a hint of peach
☆ Modelling paste: dark green, lime green, yellow, light orange, dark orange, light blue, navy blue
☆ Blue edible paste colour
☆ Sugar shaper
☆ Ball tool
☆ Craft knife
☆ 5cm (2in) circle cutter
☆ Confectioners' glaze

Cake jewellery:
Wire:
☆ Lime green bullion wire
Beads:
☆ 6mm orange and green wooden beads
☆ 6mm blue miracle beads
☆ 6mm green/pale orange glass round beads
☆ Gold and lime green Rocailles
☆ 4mm yellow gold/fire opal Swarovski crystals

Instructions:

Cover the mini-cake with sugarpaste. Thickly roll out some light blue paste, create a swirl in the paste with a ball tool then cut out with the circle cutter. Attach to one side of the top of the cake. Roll out the remaining modelling pastes between narrow spacers and cut out a selection of stripes. Attach these around the circle in a radial pattern, cutting them to fit with a craft knife. Trim the edges of the strips to create an organic shape around the circle. Using a sugar shaper fitted with a small round disc, squeeze out two navy lengths. Attach one around the central circle and the other to the outer edge of the stripes. Paint over the blue circle with diluted paste colour (see page 50). Once dry, paint over the stripes and circle with confectioners' glaze to add shine. Make a garland as shown on page 126 and place around the cake.

Key Techniques   Covering Boards (page 28); Covering Mini-Cakes (page 28); Stencilling Using Lustre Dust (page 59);

★ Diving for Pearls

Cake Jewellery chapter, page 129

★ Pink Paradise

Cake Jewellery chapter, page 130

hole with the posy pick, attach in place with sugar glue. Add the remaining layers. Create jewelled stamens using 0.5mm wire, beads and jewellery glue and, once dry, arrange inside the posy pick. Create the crown elements using the 0.5mm craft wire as described on pages 129–131. Bind the completed elements to the base wire using the 0.3mm craft wire and create a crown. Attach the crown centrally on the covered board using royal icing and allow the icing to set. Carefully position the cake in the centre of the crown and then adjust the wires as required.

★ Abstract Reasons

Cake Jewellery chapter, page 130

You will need:

- ☆ 6cm (2.5in) mini-cake
- ☆ 12.5cm (5in) hardboard cake board
- ☆ Sugarpaste: navy blue
- ☆ Modelling paste: white
- ☆ Turn of the century mini medallion stencil (DS – C334)
- ☆ Light silver edible lustre dust (SK)
- ☆ White vegetable fat (shortening)
- ☆ Cutters: flat floral set 1 (LC), Persian petal set 1 (LC), piping tube (tip) PME no. 4
- ☆ Piping tube (tip): PME no. 1
- ☆ Piping (pastry) bag
- ☆ Royal icing
- ☆ Narrow navy blue ribbon

Cake jewellery:

Wire:
- ☆ 1.5mm blue aluminium wire
- ☆ 0.3mm supa blue craft wire

Beads:
- ☆ 8mm ivory pearls
- ☆ 6mm blue miracle beads
- ☆ 6mm clear Swarovski crystals

Instructions:

Separately cover the board and cake with sugarpaste, adding the stencilled pattern to the board with the silver lustre dust. Allow to dry. Thinly roll out the white modelling paste and cut out a flat floral flower, eight small Persian petals and sixteen small circles using the piping tube (tip). Attach to the cake as shown. Create the crown as described on pages 129–131. Attach the crown centrally to the covered board, using royal icing and allow the icing to set. Carefully position the cake in the centre of the crown and then adjust the wires of the crown as necessary.

You will need:

- ☆ 6cm (2.5in) mini-cake
- ☆ 12.5cm (5in) hardboard cake board
- ☆ Posy pick
- ☆ Sugarpaste: dusky pink, white with a touch of coral
- ☆ Modelling paste: deep coral, coral, white with a touch of coral, white with a touch of dusty pink
- ☆ Cutters: large blossom (OP – F6C), 65mm (2½in) five-petal rose (FMM), 35mm (1¼in) five-petal cutter (PME), 15mm (½in) six-petal cutter (LC flat floral set 1)
- ☆ Piping tube (tip): PME no. 1, 17
- ☆ Piping (pastry) bag
- ☆ Royal icing
- ☆ Cupped flower formers
- ☆ Sugar glue
- ☆ Narrow pink ribbon

Cake jewellery:

- ☆ Jewellery glue

Wire:
- ☆ 1.5mm strong jewellery wire
- ☆ 0.5mm and 0.3mm warm silver craft wire

Beads:
- ☆ 8mm ivory pearls
- ☆ 6mm matt pink glass pearls
- ☆ 6mm pink crackle beads
- ☆ Hot pink rocailles

Instructions:

Cover the board and cake with sugarpaste and allow to dry. Insert the posy pick into the centre of the cake. Cut out flowers using the suggested modelling pastes and cutters. Remove the centre of each flower with a no. 17 piping tube (tip) then place each in a cupped former to partially dry. Once the petals hold their shape, take the largest flower and lining up the central

You will need:

- ☆ 5cm (2in) mini-cake
- ☆ Sugarpaste: pale peach
- ☆ Modelling paste: dark red, plum, purple, dusky pink, peachy pink
- ☆ Cutters: flame set (LC), curled leaf set (LC), small teardrops (LC), daisy marguerites (PME), 15mm (½in) six-petal flower (LC flat floral set 1), Indian scrolls (LC)
- ☆ Piping tubes (tips): PME no. 17, 18
- ☆ Small posy pick

Cake jewellery:

Wire:
- ☆ 0.5mm red craft wire

Beads:
- ☆ 6mm red wooden beads
- ☆ 6mm pink and amethyst crackle beads
- ☆ Purple and red rocailles
- ☆ Gold crimps

Instructions:

Cover the cake and board with sugarpaste and allow to dry. Thinly roll out the modelling pastes and cut out a selection of flowers and leaves using the suggested cutters. Attach layers of these shapes to the cake, referring to the photo. Insert the posy pick into the top of the cake. Cut out a daisy and remove a circle from the centre using a no. 17 piping tube (tip). Place on top of the cake, lining up the circle with the top of the posy pick. Create a ring of paste for the centre of the flower by cutting a circle with the no. 18 piping tube (tip) and removing the centre with the no. 17 piping tube (tip). Attach in place. Create the abstract beaded wire shapes by attaching beads to 0.5mm wire using crimps, as shown on page 130. Twist the ends of the wires together and insert into the posy pick. Adjust the arrangement as required.

★ Dotty Spotty
Colour chapter, page 43

You will need:
☆ Cupcakes baked in pink foil cases
☆ Sugarpaste: light pink, white
☆ Modelling paste: dark pink, white
☆ Round pastry cutter, same size as cupcakes
☆ Petal cutter or pointed oval cutter (LC)
☆ Piping tubes (tips): PME no. 4, 18

Instructions:
Make dotted sugarpaste and modelling paste as shown on page 43. Cut circles of sugarpaste to fit your cupcakes and decorate with petals cut from the dotted modelling paste. Top with a marbled pink-and-white ball (see page 42).

★ Out of This World
Painting chapter, page 51

You will need:
☆ Cupcakes baked in blue/green paper cases
☆ Sugarpaste: ivory
☆ Space embosser set (PC)
☆ Round pastry cutter, same size as cupcakes
☆ Ball tool
☆ Edible paste colours: selection of blues, greens, yellows, black

Instructions:
Emboss the designs onto rolled-out sugarpaste, then cut out circles to fit the top of your cupcakes. Add texture around the feet of the alien using a ball tool. Paint the designs following instructions on page 51.

★ Desert Sunrise
Painting chapter, page 52

You will need:
☆ Cupcakes baked in brown paper cases
☆ Sugarpaste: white
☆ Selection of edible paste colours
☆ Wooden dowels
☆ Round pastry cutter, same size as cupcakes

Instructions:
Roll out the white sugarpaste and print circle patterns onto the paste using wooden dowels. Then using an appropriate sized round pastry cutter, cut circles to fit the top of your cupcakes.

★ Patchwork Prints
Painting chapter, page 52

You will need:
☆ Cupcakes baked in brown paper cases
☆ Sugarpaste: ivory, orange, red
☆ Selection of edible dust colours
☆ Embossers: flower set 1 (FMM), stick embossers sets 9 and 17 (HP)
☆ Square cutter (FMM geometric set)
☆ Round pastry cutter, same size as cupcakes

Instructions:
Roll out the sugarpastes to an even thickness, ideally using spacers, and print patterns using the edible dusts. Cut a square around each design, arrange the squares on your work surface then using an appropriate sized round cutter, cut circles to fit the top of the cupcakes. Carefully attach each square in place.

★ Midas Touch
Painting chapter, page 55

You will need:
☆ Cupcakes baked in purple paper cases
☆ Sugarpaste: golden brown (use autumn leaf (SF) to colour white)
☆ Swirl cutters (PC)
☆ Round pastry cutter, same size as cupcakes
☆ Selection of edible gold lustre dusts (SK)
☆ Clear alcohol (such as gin or vodka)

Instructions:
Roll out the golden brown sugarpaste

and emboss with the swirl cutters. Using an appropriate sized round pastry cutter, cut circles to fit the top of your cupcakes. Carefully attach in place. Mix some edible gold lustre dusts with clear alcohol and paint the cupcakes as shown on page 55.

★ Love Hearts
Stencilling chapter, page 60

You will need:
☆ Cupcakes baked in purple paper cases
☆ Sugarpaste: white
☆ Edible dust colours: rose (SK), superwhite (SF)
☆ Holiday cookie tops stencil (DS)
☆ Round pastry cutter, same size as cupcakes

Instructions:
Blend the two matt dusts to make a light pink colour. Stencil the design onto the white sugarpaste and place on the top of the cupcake, as shown on page 60.

★ Perfect Peonies
Stencilling chapter, page 60

You will need:
☆ Cupcakes baked in purple paper cases
☆ Sugarpaste: white
☆ Edible dusts: pink, purple, green, white
☆ Peony cake top stencil (LC)
☆ Round pastry cutter, same size as cupcakes

Instructions:
Stencil the design onto the white sugarpaste with the different dusts and place on the top of the cupcake, as shown on page 60.

★ Tea at the Ritz
Stencilling chapter, page 62

You will need:
☆ Cupcakes baked in black and silver metallic high tea cases
☆ Sugarpaste: red with a touch of pink
☆ Royal icing
☆ Superwhite dust (SF)
☆ Winterthur heart stencil set (DS)
☆ Round pastry cutter, same size as cupcakes

Instructions:
Stencil the design onto the sugarpaste with the whitened royal icing and place on the top of the cupcake, as shown on page 62.

★ Geisha Girls
Stencilling chapter, page 65

You will need:
☆ Cupcakes baked in deep pink paper cases
☆ Sugarpaste: pink with a touch of red
☆ Royal icing: white (whitened with superwhite dust) (SF), dark pink, pink
☆ Japanese flower and scroll pattern stencils (LC)
☆ Round pastry cutter, same size as cupcakes

Instructions:
Stencil the design onto the pink sugarpaste with the different colours of royal icing as shown on page 65. Once dry, cut out circles of the appropriate size and place on top of the cupcakes.

★ Logolicious!
Stencilling chapter, page 67

You will need:
☆ Cupcakes baked in deep pink paper cases
☆ Sugarpaste: purple
☆ White vegetable fat (shortening)
☆ Homemade stencil
☆ Edible lustre dust
☆ Round pastry cutter, same size as cupcakes

Instructions:
Stencil your own design (see page 67 for how to create your own stencil) onto the purple sugarpaste using the edible lustre dust, as shown on page 59. To add interest, if desired, emboss around the stencilled pattern with an embosser (see page 87). Cut out a circle of paste and place on top of the cupcake.

Tip
Clean your stencils carefully after use and pat dry with a paper towel.

★ Love Is...
Cutters chapter, page 71

You will need:
☆ Cupcakes baked in silver foil cases
☆ Sugarpaste: black
☆ Modelling pastes: selection of pinks, light blue, orange, white
☆ Cutters: heart (LC card suit set), small stylish star (LC), piping tubes (tips) PME no. 3, 16, 17
☆ Round pastry cutter, same size as cupcakes

Instructions:
Cover the tops of the cupcakes with black sugarpaste. Marble the pink pastes (see page 42), roll out thinly and cut out hearts. Marble some orange and blue pastes, roll out thinly and cut out stars. Then thinly roll out the white, orange and blue pastes and cut out circles using the suggested piping tubes (tips). Attach the cut-out shapes to the cupcakes in the pattern of your choice.

★ Orient Express
Cutters chapter, page 73

You will need:
☆ Cupcakes baked in black paper cases
☆ Sugarpaste: white
☆ Modelling paste: black, dark pink, orange, red, coral pink
☆ Cutters: 24mm (1in) circle (FMM geometric set), five-petal flower set (PME)
☆ Ball tool and foam pad
☆ Round pastry cutter, same size as cupcakes

Instructions:
Roll out the white sugarpaste to a thickness of 5mm (³⁄₁₆in), ideally using spacers, and separately roll out the modelling pastes between narrow spacers. Using the 24mm (1in) circle cutter, cut the required shapes, as shown on page 73. Attach these shapes in place on top of the rolled-out sugarpaste. Then using a pastry cutter of an appropriate size, cut out a disc to fit the top of your cupcake. Make three cupped flowers using the five-petal flower cutter set, as shown on page 95, and layer them up on top of your cupcake. Finish off by adding a ball of paste to the centre of the flower.

★ Ever Decreasing Circles
Cutters chapter, page 74

You will need:
☆ Cupcakes baked in pink paper cases
☆ Sugarpaste: white
☆ Modelling paste: navy, dark pink, pink, white, orange, pale yellow
☆ Circle cutters (FMM geometric set)
☆ Piping tubes (tips): PME no. 4, 16, 18
☆ Round pastry cutter, same size as cupcakes

Instructions:
Cover the cupcakes with white sugarpaste. Then create the inlay work following the step-by-step instructions on page 74.

Tip
Lightly grease your work board with white vegetable fat (shortening) to prevent the paste sticking.

★ Tender Roses
Flowers chapter, page 78

You will need:
☆ Cupcakes baked in deep pink paper cases
☆ Sugarpaste: ivory
☆ Modelling paste: light pink, dark pink, purple
☆ Textured rolling pins: linen look (HP), small watermark taffeta (HP)
☆ Cutters: 1.5cm (½in) circle, daisy marguerites (PME)
☆ Round pastry cutter, same size as cupcakes

Instructions:
Roll out the sugarpaste and texture with the linen-look rolling pin (see page 88). Cut out a disc of paste using a pastry cutter of an appropriate size and attach to the top of your cupcake. Thinly roll out and texture the modelling pastes with the watermark taffeta rolling pin and use to make cut-out flowers and a selection of fabric flowers (see pages 78–79).

★ Pretty Pastels
Flowers chapter, page 79

You will need:
☆ Cupcakes baked in floral paper cases
☆ Sugarpaste: pink
☆ Modelling paste: deep pink, purple, aqua
☆ Crown embosser set (PC)
☆ Medium oval cutters set 2 (LC)
☆ Round pastry cutter, same size as cupcakes

Key Techniques   Covering Cupcakes (page 29); Cutting Out Shapes (page 71); Layering (page 72); Abutting (page 73);

Instructions:

Emboss rolled-out pink sugarpaste with the fancy scroll and heart from the crown set (see page 87). Cut out a disc of embossed paste using a pastry cutter of an appropriate size and attach to the top of your cupcake. Create a selection of fabric blossoms from the modelling paste (see page 79) and attach to the top of the cupcake as desired.

★ Darling Dahlia
Flowers chapter, page 79

You will need:
- ☆ Cupcakes baked in purple paper cases
- ☆ Sugarpaste: white
- ☆ Modelling paste: pink
- ☆ Flower embosser (PC cupcake set)
- ☆ 24mm (1in) circle cutter (FMM geometric set)
- ☆ Quilting tool (PME)
- ☆ Round pastry cutter, same size as cupcakes

Instructions:

Roll out the sugarpaste to a thickness of 5mm (³⁄₁₆in), ideally using spacers, and emboss with the flower embosser (see page 87). Cut out a disc of embossed paste using a pastry cutter of an appropriate size and attach to the top of your cupcake. Thinly roll out the modelling paste and create a fabric dahlia following the instructions on page 79. Attach to the top of the cupcake.

★ Blooming Gorgeous
Embossing chapter, page 87

You will need:
- ☆ Cupcakes baked in brown paper cases
- ☆ Sugarpaste: orange, ivory
- ☆ Modelling paste: olive green, pale olive green, pale orange, pale pink, pale blue
- ☆ Embossers: wild rose (PC), blossom and leaves – easy twist (PC)
- ☆ Paste food colours: dark orange, orange, dusky pink, olive green, green, blue
- ☆ Round pastry cutter, same size as cupcakes

Instructions:

Full instructions for these cupcakes are given on page 87.

★ Café Crème
Tools chapter, page 99

You will need:
- ☆ Cupcakes baked in brown paper cases
- ☆ Sugarpaste: light brown
- ☆ Modelling paste: golden brown
- ☆ Purple royal icing
- ☆ Multi-sized ribbon cutter (FMM)
- ☆ Paper towel
- ☆ 19.5cm (8in) French medallion stencil (DS – C144)
- ☆ Round pastry cutter, same size as cupcakes

Instructions:

Stencil the pattern onto the sugarpaste using purple royal icing (see page 62). Cut out a disc using a pastry cutter of an appropriate size and attach to the top of your cupcake. Roll out the modelling paste between narrow spacers and cut ribbons using the multi-sized ribbon cutter. Pinch the ribbons into loops, leave to fractionally harden then arrange the loops together. Position on the cupcake, adjusting the placement as necessary. Use twists of paper towel to keep the loops in place while they dry completely.

★ Rose Swirls
Piping chapter, page 105

You will need:
- ☆ Cupcakes baked in brown and gold metallic high tea cases
- ☆ Buttercream
- ☆ Orange edible paste colour
- ☆ Piping tube (tip): W – 2D
- ☆ Large piping (pastry) bag

Instructions:

Use two colours of buttercream and pipe as shown on page 105.

Tip
All the cupcake cases used in this book, and many more designs, are available from the Lindy's Cakes website.

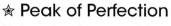

☆ Peak of Perfection
Piping chapter, page 106

You will need:
☆ Cupcakes baked in black paper cases
☆ Buttercream
☆ Piping tube (tip): W – 1E
☆ Large piping (pastry) bag
☆ Modelling paste: red, orange
☆ Pastillage: red
☆ Silicone daisy mould (Fl – FL288)
☆ Sugar shaper
☆ Rope tube (tip): PME no. 42

Instructions:
Create a pastillage shape using the sugar shaper fitted with the rope disc. Shape as desired and allow to dry. Pipe the buttercream onto the cupcakes as shown on page 106. Insert the pastillage piece and top with a moulded two-colour flower.

☆ Divine Daisies
Piping chapter, page 107

You will need:
☆ Cupcakes baked in pink and gold metallic high tea cases
☆ Buttercream
☆ Piping tube (tip): PME leaf or petal
☆ Large piping (pastry) bag
☆ Sugarpaste: pink

Instructions:
Pipe buttercream as shown on page 107 and top with a ball of pink sugarpaste.

★ Vintage Roses
Piping chapter, page 108

You will need:
☆ Cupcakes baked in blue and silver metallic high tea cases
☆ Cellophane or waxed paper squares
☆ Icing nail
☆ Buttercream
☆ Piping tube (tip): W – 103
☆ Large piping (pastry) bag
☆ Pink paste food colour

Instructions:
Colour the buttercream with the pink paste food colour. Pipe buttercream roses as shown on page 108. When sufficiently dry, transfer the roses onto the cupcakes.

★ Roses are Red...
Moulds chapter, page 115

You will need:
☆ Cupcakes baked in floral paper cases
☆ Buttercream
☆ Piping tube (tip): W – 1B
☆ Large piping (pastry) bag
☆ Roses galore mould (Fl – FL248)
☆ Rose leaf cutter (FMM)
☆ Rose leaf veiner (Gl)
☆ Edible dusts: deep red, selection of greens

Instructions:
Create a selection of roses and leaves as shown on pages 115 and 118. Dust the

roses to give the flowers depth and the leaves to bring them to life, as shown on page 118. Pipe buttercream swirls onto the cupcakes (see page 105) then add two leaves and a rose to the top of each cake.

★ Masked Marvel
Moulds chapter, page 117

You will need:
☆ Cupcakes baked in purple paper cases
☆ Piping tube (tip): W – 2D
☆ Buttercream
☆ Large piping (pastry) bag
☆ Venetian mask mould (Gl)
☆ Modelling paste: white, aqua, purple
☆ Edible paste colours
☆ Edible gold lustre dust (SK)

Instructions:
Create masks using the Venetian mask mould, as shown on page 117. Paint the design using the paste food colours and lustre dust. Pipe a swirl of buttercream onto your cupcakes. Thinly roll out small amounts of purple and aqua modelling paste. Pleat one side of each shape. Place one of each colour on the cupcakes, with the gathered edges in the centre so the pastes create a fan shape. Attach a mask to the centre.

★ Tea and Cake
Moulds chapter, page 121

You will need:
☆ Resized image

Key Techniques   Covering Cupcakes (page 29); Covering Cookies (page 29); Cutting Out Shapes (page 71);

☆ Non-toxic modelling clay
☆ Tracing paper and pencil
☆ Ball tool
☆ Dresden tool
☆ Small rose cutters (PC rose and magnolia set)
☆ Moulding gel
☆ Sugarpaste: cream
☆ DIY lace mould
☆ Modelling paste: white
☆ Selection of edible paste colours
☆ Edible bronze lustre dust
☆ Round pastry cutter, same size as cupcakes

Instructions:

Texture the cream sugarpaste with a DIY lace mould (see page 119). Using a pastry cutter of an appropriate size, cut out a disc to fit the top of your cupcake. Create a mould as shown on page 121, and use to make a white modelling paste teapot. Paint as desired with edible paste colours and bronze lustre dust and attach to the top of the cupcake.

★ Butterfly Buttons Bag

Colour chapter, page 42

You will need:

☆ Handbag cookies and cutter (LC)
☆ Sugarpaste: various blues
☆ Modelling paste: various pinks, white
☆ Cutters: 3.6cm (1½in) circle, monarch butterfly (LC), small elegant heart (LC), small paisley (LC)
☆ Piping tubes (tips): PME no. 0, 1, 3, 4, 16,18
☆ Royal icing
☆ Piping (pastry) bag

Instructions:

Cover the cookie with marbled blue sugarpaste (see page 42). Remove a large circle to create the handle. Cut a butterfly, two hearts and two paisleys from marbled pink modelling paste and small circles from white modelling paste with piping tubes (tips). Using the smallest piping tubes (tips), remove small holes from the white circles to

turn them into buttons. Cut the body away from the butterfly and recreate a butterfly on the bag using the cut-out shapes. Finish with a few piped royal icing dots using a no. 1 tube (tip).

★ Millefiori Mug

Colour chapter, page 45

You will need:

☆ Mug cookies and cutter (LC)
☆ Sugarpaste: white
☆ Modelling paste: green, lime green, white, dark pink, light pink
☆ Sugar shaper
☆ Craft knife
☆ Cutters: five-petal cutter (PME), piping tube (tip) PME no. 18

Instructions:

Roll out the white sugarpaste and cut out a mug. Cut away the handle and a flattened disc from the top of the mug and attach the body of the mug to the cookie. For the handle, cut a mug shape from thinly rolled-out white modelling paste. Take the craft knife and cut a few millimetres inside the outline of the handle to create a handle shape. Attach in place on the cookie. Create the top inside edge of the mug in the same way. Add pink trim using a sugar shaper and the small round disc. Make millefiori patterned paste as shown on page 45. Cut out petals using the five-petal cutter and attach. Cut a flower centre using the piping tube (tip) from thinly rolled-out pink modelling paste and attach.

Tip

Never be tempted to use low-calorie spreads in cookies – always use unsalted (sweet) butter.

★ Snowflake Stocking

Painting chapter, page 49

You will need:

☆ Christmas stocking cookies and cutter (LC)
☆ Sugarpaste: blue, white
☆ Edible paste colours: selection of blues
☆ Snowflake embosser (PC)
☆ Royal icing
☆ Piping (pastry) bag fitted with a coupler
☆ Piping tubes (tips): PME no. 1, 2

Instructions:

Roll out the blue sugarpaste and emboss with snowflakes (see page 87). Cut out stockings and remove the top. Place on the cookies. Allow to dry. Stipple the stockings with diluted blue edible paste colours as shown on page 49. Cut white sugarpaste stocking tops, attach in place then pipe royal icing dots in different sizes.

★ This Little Piggy

Painting chapter, page 49
You will need:

☆ Pig cookies and cutter
☆ Sugarpaste: peachy pink
☆ Pink edible paste colour
☆ Superwhite dust (SF)
☆ Natural sponges
☆ Dresden tool

Instructions:

Cut out pigs from peachy pink sugarpaste and attach to the pig cookies. Use a Dresden tool to define the legs, snout, eats and eye. Add a curly tail. Allow to dry. Sponge paint as shown on page 49.

Dresden Tool (page 94); Sugar Shaper (pages 96–98); Piping Swirls (page 105); Piping Dots (page 109); Two-Colour Moulding (page 116)

✿ An Apple a Day
Painting chapter, page 50

You will need:
☆ Apple cookies and cutter
☆ Sugarpaste: green, brown
☆ Modelling paste: green
☆ Rose leaf cutter (FMM)
☆ Rose leaf veiner (GI)
☆ Dresden tool
☆ Edible paste colours: selection of greens, red
☆ Superwhite dust (SF)

Instructions:
Cut out apples from green sugarpaste, remove the stalk, leaf and blossom end and attach to the cookies. Model a stalk from brown paste. Add a small ball of brown paste for the blossom end and texture with the pointed end of a Dresden tool. Cut and vein a leaf (see page 118). Paint the apple as shown on page 50.

★ Killer Heels
Painting chapter, page 50

You will need:
☆ High heel cookies and cutter (LC)
☆ Sugarpaste: white
☆ Modelling paste: black
☆ Lace
☆ Cutting wheel (PME)
☆ Craft knife
☆ Black edible paste colour
☆ Clear alcohol (such as gin or vodka)
☆ Paper towel

Instructions:
Roll out the white sugarpaste and texture with lace (see page 90). Cut out shoe shapes and attach to the cookies. Mark the line between the heel and the shoe with a cutting wheel. Using a craft knife, cut away the tip of the heel and the sole of the shoe, followed by a thin tapered strip from the top of the shoe – this area will form the lining of shoe. Paint as shown on page 50 then replace the cut-away sections with black modelling paste.

★ Bottle of Bubbly
Painting chapter, page 55

You will need:
☆ Champagne bottle cookie and cutter (LC)
☆ Sugarpaste: green, golden brown
☆ Modelling paste: white
☆ Dresden tool
☆ Embossers: scroll (FMM), nursery set 12 (HP)
☆ Edible pens
☆ Edible gold leaf
☆ Edible gold lustre dust (SK)
☆ Clear alcohol (such as gin or vodka)

Instructions:
Cover the bottle using green sugarpaste and the top using golden brown sugarpaste. Indent the cork with the end of a Dresden tool. Add the gold leaf to the top, as shown on page 55. Cut out labels from thinly rolled-out modelling paste and emboss as desired. Attach in place. Use edible pens to add details to the labels and edible lustre dust mixed with clear alcohol to add highlights.

★ Silver Swirls
Stencilling chapter, page 59

You will need:
☆ Heart cookies and cutter (W nesting hearts)
☆ Sugarpaste: pink
☆ Snowflake edible lustre dust (SK)
☆ Contemporary valentine heart cookie top stencil set (DS)
☆ White vegetable fat (shortening)

Instructions:
Stencil the design onto the pink sugarpaste with the metallic dust and place on the top of the cookie, as shown on page 59.

★ Wonky Wedding
Stencilling chapter, page 61

You will need:
☆ Wonky wedding cake cookies and cutter (LC)
☆ Sugarpaste: deep purple, claret, lilac
☆ Royal icing: lilac, tint of pink, purple
☆ Stencils: winterthur heart set (DS), chinese floral circle (LC)

Instructions:
Stencil and attach one tier at a time using different colours of sugarpaste and royal icing for each tier, as shown on page 61.

Key Techniques Covering Cookies (page 29); Stencilling (pages 59–67); Cutting Out Shapes (page 71);

★ Designer Daisies
Stencilling chapter, page 66

You will need:

☆ Swimming costume cookies and cutter (LC)
☆ Sugarpaste: black, red
☆ Modelling paste: red, pink, black
☆ Pink royal icing
☆ Flower scroll stencil (DS)
☆ Daisy marguerite cutters (PME)
☆ Piping tubes (tips): PME no. 16, 17

Instructions:

Stencil the design onto the black sugarpaste with the pink royal icing (see page 61) and place on top of the cookie. Cut a small ball of paste in half and attach the halves to the chest area to give more shape. Cut the top of the swimsuit from the red sugarpaste then embellish the design with cut-out daisies, as shown on page 66.

★ Tiers of Joy
Stencilling chapter, page 66

You will need:

☆ Wedding cake cookies and cutter (LC)
☆ Sugarpaste: pink with a touch of red, white
☆ Royal icing
☆ Superwhite dust (SF)
☆ Card or waxed paper
☆ Craft knife
☆ Paper punch
☆ Edible dust colours

Instructions:

Create your own stencils from the card or waxed paper (see page 66). Stencil your designs onto the sugarpastes with whitened royal icing and edible dusts and place on top of the different tiers of the cookie.

★ Funky Flip Flops
Stencilling chapter, page 67

You will need:

☆ Flip flop cookies and cutter (LC)
☆ Sugarpaste: deep pink
☆ Modelling paste: purple, white, light pink
☆ Greek repeat pattern stencil (LC)
☆ Mini flower mould (FI – FL107)

Instructions:

Emboss the design onto the deep pink sugarpaste, as shown on page 67, and place on the top of the cookies. To make the straps, cut 1cm (⅜in) wide strips of purple modelling paste and mitre one end of each. Take a mitred end and attach about halfway down the foot. Twist the strip 180 degrees towards the centre of the shoe, position the twisted strip so the strap finishes between the toes and cut off the excess paste. Repeat for second strap. Add a two-colour moulded modelling paste flower to cover the join.

★ Wedding Waistcoat
Embossing chapter, page 87

You will need:

☆ Waistcoat cookies and cutter (LC)
☆ Sugarpaste: golden brown
☆ Modelling paste: white, ivory
☆ Dresden tool
☆ Cutting wheel (PME)
☆ Craft knife
☆ Leaf embosser (HP spring set 9)
☆ Piping tube (tip): PME no. 4

Instructions:

Thinly roll out the white modelling paste and cut out a triangle for the front of the shirt. Attach in place then add two smaller, thicker triangles for the collar. Cut a diamond from ivory paste and attach to the cookie to create the cravat. Add a ball of ivory paste for the knot. Add movement to the paste with a Dresden tool. Roll out the sugarpaste to a 5mm (³⁄₁₆in) thickness, ideally using spacers, and emboss with the leaf embosser. Cut out the waistcoat using the cookie cutter and remove a triangle of paste from the front. Attach to the cookie. Add opening and button details using a cutting wheel and piping tube (tip).

★ Bridal Blooms
Embossing chapter, page 88

You will need:

☆ Wedding cake cookies and cutter (LC)
☆ Sugarpaste: three shades of pink
☆ Flat floral cutter set 2 (LC)
☆ Daisy centre stamp (JEM)
☆ Dresden tool

Instructions:

Roll out the sugarpaste colours to a 5mm (³⁄₁₆in) thickness, ideally using spacers, and emboss using the flat floral cutter (see page 88). Cut out cake shapes then cut across the base of each tier to separate the tiers. Attach tiers of different colours to the cookies. Emboss the centre of each flower with a daisy centre stamp then indent the petals with the narrow end of a Dresden tool.

Small-Scale Embossers (page 87); Dresden Tool (page 94); Cutting Wheel (page 89); Two-Colour Moulding (page 116)

★ Wonderful Wellies
Embossing chapter, page 89

You will need:
☆ Double welly cookies and wellie cutter (LC)
☆ Sugarpaste: ivory, pink, green
☆ Embossers: rose and magnolia (PC),
   wild rose (for leaves) (PC)
☆ Cutting wheel (PME)
☆ Craft knife
☆ Dresden tool
☆ Small oval cutter (LC set 1)
☆ Edible paste colours: pink, green

Instructions:
Create double welly cookies using the welly cutter by abutting a complete welly dough shape with a partial welly dough shape – the two will bake to form one cookie. Cover and emboss the back welly first, using paste slightly thinner than 5mm (³⁄₁₆in). Use the rose embossers to add a floral pattern (see page 87). Then add embossed lines using a cutting wheel. Add and texture the front welly. If desired, make the top, buckles, soles and heels in a contrasting colour, cutting the buckle surround with a small oval cutter and embossing the soles with a Dresden tool. Paint over the embossed floral pattern with diluted edible paste colours.

Tip
When painting over the pattern, let the pink flowers dry completely before adding the green leaves.

★ Haute-Couture Heels
Embossing chapter, page 89

You will need:
☆ Platform stiletto cookies and cutter (LC)
☆ Sugarpaste: black, dusky claret
☆ Flat floral cutter set 1 (LC)
☆ Embroidery embosser (PC)
☆ Cutting wheel (PME)
☆ Ball tool

Instructions:
Roll out the two sugarpaste colours and cut out a shoe shape from each using the cookie cutter. Referring to the photo, cut out the shoe upper from the pink paste and attach to the cookie. Emboss the flowers with a cutter (see page 88) and indent each petal with the small end of a ball tool (see page 89). Add a stripe of black sugarpaste to the base of the sole, follow this with an embossed pink strip and finish off with black. Add a black heel and instep to complete.

★ Everything's Rosy
Embossing chapter, page 89

You will need:
☆ Cushion cookies and cutter (LC)
☆ Sugarpaste: white
☆ Modelling paste: pale pink, pale green
☆ Tea rose embosser (PC)
☆ Piping tubes (tips): PME no. 4, 16, 17, 18
☆ Edible paste colours: pink, green, black

Instructions:
Cover the cookie with white sugarpaste and emboss rows of circles using piping tubes (tips), as shown on page 89. Roll out the modelling pastes very thinly and emboss and cut out the rose and leaves from the pink and green pastes (see page 87). Apply colour to the circles and rose using diluted edible paste colours.

★ Glamorous Gown
Tools chapter, page 94

You will need:
☆ Fitted dress cookies and cutter (LC)
☆ Sugarpaste: peachy pink
☆ Modelling paste: ivory
☆ Dresden tool
☆ Moroccan mosaic craft punch (Xcut)

Instructions:
Roll a small ball of sugarpaste and cut in half. Attach each half to the chest area of the cookie to give shape to the dress. Roll out the pink sugarpaste and cut out the dress. Cut away the very top section of the dress to make it strapless and attach to the cookie, smoothing the paste over the chest. Create movement in the skirt by stroking the paste with a finger. Cut another dress from the sugarpaste and cut out the draped fabric shapes. Place the two sections of drape onto the cookie and texture with a Dresden tool (see page 94). Create a belt using a punch and modelling paste (see page 101) and attach in place.

★ Hot Pink Heels
Tools chapter, page 97

You will need:
☆ Platform stiletto cookies and cutter (LC)
☆ Sugarpaste: pink
☆ Modelling paste: pink
☆ Cutting wheel (PME)
☆ Craft knife
☆ Dresden tool
☆ Sugar shaper

Instructions:
Roll out the pink sugarpaste and cut a shoe. Separately cut the heel, sole and straps from the shape and attach to the cookie as shown. Mark the tip of the heel and sole of the shoe with a cutting wheel (see page 89). Indent eyelets with the pointed end of a Dresden tool. Using a sugar shaper, the small round disc and pink modelling paste, squeeze out lengths of paste (see page 97). Attach a length to the sole of the shoe, short lace lengths from each eyelet and finish off with a bow, as shown.

★ Teatime Treat
Tools chapter, page 98

You will need:
☆ Teapot cookies and cutter
☆ Sugarpaste: ivory
☆ Modelling paste: deep pink, light pink, dark green, lime green, orange, brown, ivory
☆ Piping tube (tip): PME no. 18
☆ Sugar shaper
☆ Cutting wheel (PME)

Instructions:
Roll out the sugarpaste to a 5mm (³⁄₁₆in) thickness, ideally using spacers, and cut out a teapot. Cut away the handle area and the base and attach the body and spout to the cookie. Define the join between the body and spout with a cutting wheel (see page 89). For the handle, roll a sausage of sugarpaste and attach in place as shown. Create a pink modelling paste rope using the sugar shaper and the small rope disc (see page 98). Cut the rope in half and attach one half to the base of the teapot and the other half to the top of the pot to create the rim of the lid. Trim to size. Decorate the teapot with polka dots cut from thinly rolled-out modelling paste, using the piping tube (tip) (see page 71). Finally, roll a ball of pink paste and attach to the top of the pot.

★ Kitten Heels
Tools chapter, page 99

You will need:
☆ Kitten heel cookies and cutter (LC)
☆ Sugarpaste: purple, light brown
☆ Modelling paste: purple, dark brown
☆ Cutting wheel (PME)
☆ Craft knife

Instructions:
Roll out the light brown sugarpaste and cut out a shoe. Cut away the heel then attach the remaining paste to the cookie. Thinly roll out the dark brown modelling paste and cut freehand animal print shapes with a cutting wheel. Attach the shapes to the shoe. Cut a heel from purple sugarpaste using the cookie cutter and a cutting wheel and attach in place. Add a brown tip to the heel. Cut a thin strip of brown modelling paste and add to the bottom of the shoe to create a sole. Trim the top of the shoe with a strip of purple modelling paste. Finally add a purple loop and flattened ball for the bow.

★ Whole Lotta Dots
Piping chapter, page 109

You will need:
☆ Heart and pram cookies and cutters (LC)
☆ Sugarpaste: teal, light teal, pink, flesh
☆ Modelling paste: pink, dark brown
☆ Piping tubes (tips): PME no. 1, 1.5, 2
☆ Modern flowers stencil (DS – C559)
☆ Cutters: set of round pastry cutters, daisy marguerites (PME)
☆ Royal icing
☆ Superwhite dust (SF)
☆ Teal edible paste colour
☆ Piping (pastry) bag and coupler

Instructions:
Stencil freshly rolled-out sugarpaste using the modern flowers stencils and appropriately coloured royal icing (see page 61). Cut out hearts and sections of the pram and add to the cookies before the royal icing sets. Add light teal sugarpaste wheels, using the pastry cutters to cut these out, and a handle. Indent each wheel with a slightly smaller circle. Using the flesh sugarpaste, cut and add a circle for the baby's head, then add a smile using the wide end of a piping tube (tip) and add eyes with a cocktail stick (toothpick). Model a curl of brown modelling paste for hair and cut pink modelling paste flowers for the wheel spokes. Add piped royal icing dots, as shown on page 109.

Dresden Tool (page 94); Tools as Embossers (page 89); Cutting Wheel (page 99); Sugar Shaper (pages 96–98); Piping Dots (page 109)

★ Baby Booties

Piping chapter, page 110

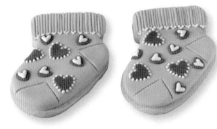

You will need:

☆ Baby sock cookies and cutters (LC)
☆ Sugarpaste: pink
☆ Modelling paste: dark pink
☆ Palette knife
☆ Quilting tool (PME)
☆ Small heart plunger cutters (PME)
☆ Royal icing
☆ Piping tube (tip): PME no. 1
☆ Piping (pastry) bag
☆ Superwhite dust (SF)

Instructions:

Cut out socks from the pink sugarpaste. Cut away the tops of the socks and add vertical lines using a palette knife. Attach both sections of the socks to the cookies then define the toe and heel sections with a quilting tool. Add a selection of small hearts cut from dark pink modelling paste. Finally pipe dots and hearts with whitened royal icing as shown on pages 109–110.

★ Monochrome Mugs

Piping chapter, page 111

You will need:

☆ Mug cookies and cutters (LC)
☆ Sugarpaste: black, white
☆ Art Nouveau tulip embosser (PC)
☆ Craft knife

☆ Royal icing
☆ Piping tube (tip): PME no. 2
☆ Piping (pastry) bags
☆ Superwhite dust (SF)
☆ Black edible paste colour

Instructions:

Follow the instructions on page 111 to create these cookies, using black and white sugarpaste and royal icing.

★ Flowery Flip Flops

Moulds chapter, page 116

You will need:

☆ Flip flop cookies and cutter (LC)
☆ Sugarpaste: aqua
☆ Modelling paste: jade green, white, yellow
☆ Daisy chain embosser (PC)
☆ Daisy mould set (FI – FL288)
☆ Multi-sized ribbon cutter (FMM)

Instructions:

Emboss the daisy design onto the sugarpaste, as shown on page 87. Cut out flip flops from this paste using the cookie cutter and place on the top of the cookies. To make the straps, cut 1cm (⅜in) wide strips of modelling paste and mitre one end of each. Take a mitred end and attach about halfway down the foot. Twist the strip 180 degrees towards the centre of the shoe, position the twisted strip so the strap finishes between the toes and cut off the excess paste. Repeat for the second flip flop strap. Add a two-colour moulded daisy to cover the join, as shown on page 116.

★ Christmas Crackers

Moulds chapter, page 119

You will need:

☆ Cracker cookies and cutter (LC)
☆ Pastillage
☆ Lace or textured wallpaper
☆ Sugarpaste: purple, golden brown
☆ Modelling paste: red, purple
☆ Cutting wheel (PME)
☆ Dresden tool
☆ Small flower mould (FI – FL127)
☆ Edible paste/dust colours

Instructions:

Make a pastillage mould as shown on page 119 and use to emboss your sugarpaste. Cut out crackers from the sugarpaste using the cookie cutter and attach to the cookies. Mark the gathered sections on the crackers using a cutting wheel (see pages 89) and a Dresden tool. Add strips of red modelling paste to the gathered sections and create red ribbons for the centre decoration. Attach a two-colour moulded flower (see page 116) in the centre. Use edible paste or dust colours to highlight the embossed design as desired.

Tip

For a shiny metallic finish, mix edible lustre dust with confectioners' glaze and use as paint.

Key Techniques Covering Cookies (page 29); Dresden Tool (page 94); Piping Hearts (page 110); Brushwork Embroidery (page 111)

Templates

Gaudi's Grandeur – Tools chapter

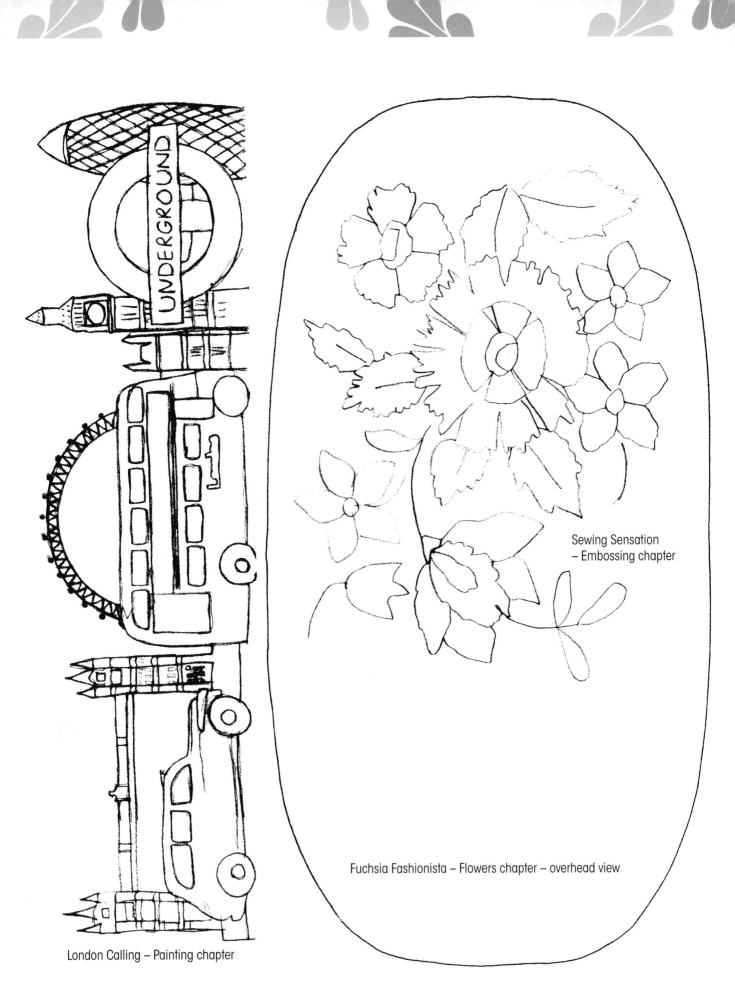

Sewing Sensation
– Embossing chapter

Fuchsia Fashionista – Flowers chapter – overhead view

London Calling – Painting chapter

Fuchsia Fashionista
– Flowers chapter
– curved pieces

Coral Creation
– Piping chapter

Tea and Cake
– Moulds chapter

Fuchsia Fashionista
– Flowers chapter
– front view

Patchwork Heart
– Colour chapter

Fuchsia Fashionista – Flowers
chapter – side view

Acknowledgments

I'd like to thank my team at Lindy's Cakes for helping make everything possible. Without their support I would not have the freedom to be creative or the time to write – my life simply would not be half as exciting or fulfilled. Special thanks go to my husband Graham, who as well as being a major part of 'Team Lindy' is always there to share the challenges of running a business and writing a book simultaneously. A huge thank you!

Thanks also go to the various manufacturers, without whose products this book would not have been so easy to write. Good products take time, effort and resources, yet they are vital to the continuation and development of our craft.

Thanks must also go to the book's two photographers, Simon Whitmore, whose stunning photographs make this book so stylish and contemporary and Karl Adamson whose skill and attention to detail in all the step photography means that the techniques all flow beautifully and are easy to follow.

Finally, I'd like to thank all my enthusiastic students, customers, Facebook fans and Twitter and blog followers, whose many and varied comments and questions are so helpful when it comes to writing books.

About the Author

Well known, and highly respected in the Sugarcraft industry, Lindy Smith has over 20 years experience in sugarcrafting. Lindy is a designer, who likes to share her love of sugarcraft and inspire fellow enthusiasts by writing books and teaching. Lindy is the author of seven cake decorating titles for D&C: *Creative Celebration Cakes, Storybook Cakes, Celebrate with a Cake!, Party Animal Cakes, Cakes to Inspire and Desire, Bake Me I'm Yours... Cookie* and *Bake Me I'm Yours... Cupcake Celebration.*

Lindy's teaching takes her all around the world, giving her the opportunity to educate and inspire while also learning about local traditions and cake-decorating issues. This knowledge is ultimately then fed back into her work. She has appeared on television and presented a sugarcraft series on *Good Food Live.*

Lindy also heads Lindy's Cakes Ltd, a well-established business that runs her online shop www.lindyscakes.co.uk, and her cake decorating workshops both in the UK and abroad. To see what Lindy is currently doing, become a fan of Lindy's Cakes on Facebook or follow Lindy on Twitter. For baking advice and a wealth of information visit her blog, via the Lindy's Cakes website: **www.lindyscakes.co.uk**.

Suppliers

UK

Lindy's Cakes Ltd (LC)
Unit 2, Station Approach, Wendover
Buckinghamshire HP22 6BN
Tel: +44 (0)1296 622418
www.lindyscakes.co.uk
*Online shop for products and equipment used in this
and Lindy's other books, including Lindy's own ranges
of cutters and stencils*

Alan Silverwood Ltd
Ledsam House, Ledsam Street
Birmingham B16 8DN
Tel: +44 (0)121 454 3571
www.alansilverwood.co.uk
*Manufacturer of multi-sized cake pan, multi mini cake
pans and spherical moulds/ball tins*

Ceefor Cakes
PO Box 443, Leighton Buzzard
Bedforshire LU7 1AJ
Tel: +44 (0)1525 375237
www.ceeforcakes.co.uk
Supplier of strong cake boxes – most sizes available

FMM Sugarcraft (FMM)
Unit 7, Chancerygate Business Park, Whiteleaf Road,
Hemel Hempstead, Hertfordshire HP3 9HD
Tel: +44 (0)1442 292970
www.fmmsugarcraft.com
Manufacturer of cutters

Holly Products (HP)
Primrose Cottage, Church Walk, Norton in Hales
Shropshire, TF9 4QX
Tel: +44 (0)1630 655759
www.hollyproducts.co.uk
Manufacturer and supplier of embossing sticks and moulds

M&B Specialised Confectioners Ltd
3a Millmead Estate, Mill Mead Road
London N17 9ND
Tel: +44 (0)208 801 7948
www.mbsc.co.uk
Manufacturer and supplier of sugarpaste

Patchwork Cutters (PC)
Unit 12, Arrowe Commercial Park, Arrowe Brook Road, Upton
Wirral CH49 1AB
Tel: +44 (0)151 678 5053
www.patchworkcutters.co.uk
Manufacturer and supplier of cutters and embossers

US

Global Sugar Art
625 Route 3, Unit 3
Plattsburgh, NY 12901
Tel: 1-518-561-3039 or 1-800-420-6088 (toll free)
www.globalsugarart.com
Sugarcraft supplier that imports many UK products to the US

Cake Craft Shoppe
3530 Highway 6
Sugar Land, TX 77478
Tel: 1-281-491-3920
www.cakecraftshoppe.com
Sugarcraft supplier

First Impressions Molds
300 Business Park Way, Suite A-200
Royal Palm Beach, FL 33411
Tel: 1-561-784-7186
www.firstimpressionsmolds.com
Manufacturer and supplier of moulds

Australia

Iced Affair
53 Church Street
Camperdown NSW 2050
Tel: +61 (0)2 9519 3679
www.icedaffair.com.au
Sugarcraft supplier

Abbreviations used in this book

DS – Designer Stencils
FI – First Impressions
FMM – FMM Sugarcraft
GI – Great Impressions
HP – Holly Products
JEM – JEM Cutters
LC – Lindy's Cakes Ltd
PC – Patchwork Cutters
PME – PME Sugarcraft
SF – Sugarflair
SK – Squires Kitchen
W – Wilton

Index